To the man or woman caught in the whirlpool of depression, victory seems an impossible goal to reach. To these same people comes the joyful news that there is an answer.

Here are the keys to a life of freedom, peace of mind, and abundant happiness.

There is victory over depression!

Victory over Depression

by Bert Allbritton

PITTSBURGH AND COLFAX STREETS, SPRINGDALE, PA. 15144

VICTORY OVER DEPRESSION

Bert Allbritton
10345 Webbs Chapel Road
Dallas, Texas 75229

Copyright © 1981 by Bert Allbritton
Printed in the United States of America
ISBN: 0-88368-104-8

All rights reserved. No portion of this book may be used without written permission of the publisher, with the exception of brief excerpts in magazine articles, reviews, etc. For information, address Whitaker House, Pittsburgh and Colfax Streets, Springdale, Pennsylvania 15144.

Scripture quotations are from the *New American Standard Bible*, © The Lockman Foundation 1960, 1962, 1963, 1968, 1971, 1972, 1973, 1975. Used by permission.

CONTENTS

Foreword by Pat Boone

One:	What is Depression?	15
Two:	The Causes of Depression	20
Three:	Disappointment and Rejection	29
Four:	The Dangers of Self-Hate	37
Five:	The Dangers of Unfair Comparison	43
Six:	Sin or Sickness?	51
Seven:	Elijah's Depression	57
Eight:	Jonah's Pit	67
Nine:	The Depression of David	82
Ten:	Yesterday and Tomorrow	91
Eleven:	Depressing Associations	103
Twelve:	Obtaining the Victory	111

FOREWORD

"My friend was quite wealthy, the son of a prominent California family. He grew up accustomed to having anything that he wanted, and even now was married to a beautiful young woman and was the father of two handsome young sons. He was 32 years old, and involved in a number of active and successful businesses.

Late one morning, he stepped into the study of his sumptuous home, closed the door, scribbled a note—and shot himself in the head.

All of us were stunned, and we asked the only question we could think of: "Why?" The answer, the one and only answer—depression.

My friend had everything to live for, no real or drastic problems. But his perspective on life was warped, and he was subject to this deep and often irrational malady. Depression, as I understand it, doesn't have to be grounded in real problems. Though it can be precipitated or aggravated by serious difficulties, often it is almost inexplainable and apparently without serious cause.

It just is—and it wounds, inhibits, distorts and destroys.

Other books have been written about depression, and some of them by real experts, fellows with degrees in psychology, medicine and different kinds of professional counseling.

Bert Allbritton is none of the above—he's a pastor.

But a pastor deals with people who are at the end of their ropes, people who sense that theirs is more than a physical or emotional or economic need, people who are "sick of soul." Bert has been trained and accredited by the Holy Spirit, and his source material is The Creator's Handbook. He's had to help people, firsthand, who perhaps couldn't afford high priced psychiatrists, and for whom there was no medical or "scientific" help available. And he has become something of an expert in the field.

Personally, I've benefited greatly by reading this book. I want to give it to friends that I know are grappling with depression right now, and I intend to keep several on hand for "first aid" in the future. The reason this book is so effective is that it is so full of Scripture, and there is no remedy for any ailment that can equal the Word of God.

Jesus, the Great Physician, had none of the world's credentials, but He healed all who came to

Him, whether their affliction was spiritual, emotional, or physical. He laid the groundwork and established the authority for His ministry in the fourth chapter of Luke, when He quoted part of Isaiah 61:

> "The Spirit of the Lord God is upon me; because the Lord hath anointed me to preach good tidings unto the meek; *He hath sent me to bind up the broken hearted*, to proclaim liberty to the captives, and the opening of the prison to them that are bound; To proclaim the acceptable year of the Lord, and the day of vengeance of our God; to comfort all that mourn; To appoint unto them that mourn in Zion, to give unto them beauty for ashes, *the oil of joy for mourning, the garment of praise for the spirit of heaviness:* that they might be called trees of righteousness, the planting of the Lord, that He might be glorified" (Isaiah 61:1-3).

God bless Bert Allbritton, and all who read this book, for surely anyone who focuses his attention on the Lord Jesus Christ and His Word will become immune to the deadly malady called depression.

Pat Boone
Beverly Hills, California

DEDICATION

Affectionately dedicated...to my wife, Norma Jean, who has untiringly, unselfishly and lovingly labored with me for these many years. She insisted that I finish this book, for she believed this message needed to be heard.

...And to the many depressed people that I believe will be helped by this book.

Victory over Depression

CHAPTER ONE

WHAT IS DEPRESSION?

Ask a dozen people for a definition of depression, and you'll likely receive a dozen answers, all different, yet all strangely similar.

It is the feeling of loneliness, one will say. It is frustration, helplessness, despair and emptiness, says another. It is like your insides are caved in and everything seems hopeless. It is paralyzing fear, mental panic and desperate retreat, all in one, and still the descriptions are not exhausted.

Depression is the anxiety of the troubled man who visited a psychiatrist only to be told to attend a famous clown act playing nearby.

"It will make you laugh," said the psychiatrist. "That's what you need—a good hearty laugh."

"I'll go, but it won't help me," said the discouraged patient. "I'm the clown."

For people who know it as well as the clown, depression seems inescapable. It returns like a circling vulture to undermine ambition, sap vitality and weaken emotional stability. Depression may lift as suddenly as it arrived, but scarcely ever without leaving behind that dangerous, tormenting, haunting thought: "Sure, I'm free now. But for how long?"

What an enemy! What a tragic waste of energy and lives!

Who can suffer from depression? Every individual is a target at one time or another. Doctors and ministers counsel with women two or three times more often than with men, but men are more susceptible to alcohol, and their suicide rate is three times greater. So, though more women are victims of depression than men, women apparently cope with it better.

Can depression be "cured"? I can give a resounding "yes!" to that question for several reasons.

First of all, although depression is increasing in tendency and intensity in twentieth century America, there is more medical, scientific and spiritual help available now than ever before. Physicians, ministers, psychologists, psychiatrists and social workers are all in the business of helping people whip the causes and symptoms of depression.

But depression is curable for yet another, more important reason. Jesus, the great Healer, still delivers depressed spirits today. Even after Christ's resurrection from the dead and ascension into heaven, the apostle Peter was reminding his congregation "of Jesus of Nazareth, how God anointed Him with the Holy Spirit, and with power, and how He went about doing good, and healing all that were oppressed by the devil; for God was with Him" (Acts 10:38).

What Jesus accomplished with power centuries ago, He can do today, for He is the same yesterday, today and forever (Hebrews 13:8).

The Symptoms of Depression

Those who know depression firsthand know its symptoms as well as they know the alphabet. But everyone should be familiar with its most common signs and be prepared to address them when they appear in the lives of family members, co-workers or associates.

It is important to know how the depressed person feels inside. With depression comes a loss of perception and, sometimes, judgment. With it comes an inner hurt that goes far deeper than unhappiness and colors the way a person looks at life and his surroundings. Hopelessness, despair, sadness, apathy and gloom are the spiritual and emotional cultures upon which depression thrives.

In a period of depression, sexual interest wanes and is replaced by a sense of deep unworthiness. Some people may gorge themselves on food, while others lose their appetites entirely. Some victims sleep constantly, while others cannot sleep at all. Self-esteem slips as a person feels less and less positive about himself and his abilities.

As depression deepens, it brings a strong desire to escape from problems, and even from life itself. *Escape* becomes an encompassing drive—to escape the lowliness, rejection, loneliness and hopelessness which tear the human spirit. It is a sad fact that many depressed people lose their will to live. We may see them with a smile on their lips, but we can hardly suspect the tormenting pain that stabs their hearts, edging them to the exits of life.

Understandably, depression brings an oversensitivity to the actions, gestures and comments of others. Every remark by another person, even casual teasing and sideways glances, becomes fuel for thought to the depressed person. And like a dentist who hits upon an exposed nerve, the depressed individual is always ready to jump on any misunderstood statement or misinterpreted action to reinforce his negative self-concepts. The sufferer becomes irritable and cries easily, and often has trouble controlling his other emotions, especially anger. Always present is an underlying sense of guilt, either real or imagined or both, it doesn't matter. Some even experience deep guilt because they are depressed and wonder if something is wrong with them. Like a judge who has rapped his wooden gavel on a heavy bench, the word "guilty" echoes from one mental wall to another, sometimes driving the suffering individual out of his mind.

A depressed person is rarely ever free from this sense of guilt. He feels helpless, capable of accomplishing nothing, and turns to others. While the apostle Paul wrote, "I can do all things through Christ which strengthens me," a depressed person can become overly dependent on other people, which only reinforces his sense of self-worthlessness.

How damaging is depression? As a young man I had a real desire to become a medical doctor. I have long admired men and women who can diagnose sickness, administer treatment, and bring healing. Now, however, I'm grateful God called me to minister healing of another sort: the healing of emotions and spirits. For just as cancer can eat tissues and destroy lives, so depression can cripple and kill from within. If physical healing is important, then spiritual healing is more so, for it is the spiritual man who lives forever.

I believe emotional and spiritual depression can be broken. I believe with the Psalmist that every individual can say, "This is the day which the Lord hath made; we will rejoice and be glad in it" (Psalm 118:24). I believe that life is good, for everything God created was created in loving perfection. God made each day a good day for living, for every one of us.

CHAPTER TWO

THE CAUSES OF DEPRESSION

Depression has a quiver full of natural causes, some so simple that we tend to overlook them. In thousands of cases it surfaces through the little irritations of life that become enlarged by fear, pain and self-doubt.

Emotional stress is one such understandable trigger for depression. The sudden trauma of very bad news or severe disappointment can release a clutching sense of loneliness, despair, and vulnerability. So can personal failure to reach an important goal. So can divorce, financial reverse, or the crushing loss of a loved one. Depression can settle into place through an inability to overcome the tugs, pushes and tears of daily living.

Physical problems can cause depression as well. In fact, the body, spirit and mind are so united and intertwined that they generally affect each other within seconds. The problem is two-fold: physical problems cause depression, and depression causes physical problems. When the body hurts, people become irritable and the thinking processes slow down.

Several years ago, I suffered from low blood sugar. When my body's sugar level was low, I became depressed. Small tasks turned into major ones, simple routines became drudgery. On days my body suffered, I felt tired, physically drained, and bored with my usual daily challenges.

How easily my physical condition affected my emotional and spiritual outlook, and how quickly a few bites of sugar sweetened my entire day!

Even more serious was a disease I contacted while serving in the Navy during World War II. A military doctor said the disease was incurable, and I was shipped home to die. On the doctor's orders, I was discharged from the Navy with a 100 percent disability. I was frightened and alone. My mind couldn't shake the thought of death, and my spirit sank into depression. I felt helpless and forgotten, like a wasted victim of circumstance when I was scarcely twenty years old.

Then after coming to Christ, a startling thing happened. I prayed for my hopeless situation, and my physical condition began to change. The symptoms dwindled. I felt better. My faith grew as my depression melted. Before long my disability was changed to zero percent, and I was completely healed, both in body and spirit.

Always let the search for the cause of depression

include a physical checkup!

Depression often has its beginning from an inherited or learned disposition to look on the dark side of life. Whether it is an inborn tendency or one learned in the environment of childhood, I cannot say, but it is startling to note that thousands of people who give place to the negative thoughts of doubt, fear and death—who let such thoughts prey upon their minds—later complain of depression. There is an important connection between self-conception and depression, as we will later see.

Separation From God

Perhaps the most common form of spiritual and emotional depression has its roots in a single tragic malady: separation from God. The spirit of man was created to enjoy life-sustaining fellowship with his Creator, a spiritual relationship as important and necessary as food and sleep. Just as automobiles were created to drive on roadways, so was man created for a designed purpose and destiny.

Sin broke that unity with God and distorted His purpose for our lives. Only through the death of Christ at Calvary are we reconciled with Him again, if we believe Him and receive His provision for our reconciliation. Only then can we receive His promised peace.

Men, women and children who have not

experienced the forgiveness of Christ will never know true fulfillment and satisfaction in life. Their spiritual "malnourishment" brings emotional stress, confusion and emptiness that eventually erupts in anger, despair or even depression. Under it all lies an explainable sense of guilt and restlessness, for the heart of man can never find rest, until it finds rest in God.

Before my personal surrender to Jesus Christ, I knew such depression and guilt. There were many days during World War II that I thought of little else but eternity. I recalled the words to a simple chorus we had sung in church back home: "Eternity, Eternity, where will you spend Eternity?" How terrible to die on some desolate beach or wide expanse of ocean and not know God, I thought. How wasted a life. How wasted a mother's prayers!

I struggled in my guilt, still unable to say yes to God. But God was listening to my mother's prayers, for one day, shortly before my submarine sailed out of port, I was transferred. The submarine sailed without me. Several days later, I learned my submarine and crew has been torpedoed. I heard that all aboard were lost.

No altar call could have drawn me more surely to Christ than did that encounter with death. Again, my mind spoke the words, "Where will you spend Eternity?" There was a truth in the words to that song that I could not avoid. My heart felt heavy; my spirit sank; and I realized I was disobeying a loving, merciful God simply because I had not responded to His open arms.

Shortly after this, I contracted the tropical disease that I mentioned earlier in the chapter. I was transferred from one Navy hospital to another before being sent home with all hope gone.

At home, and down to 135 pounds, I went to church with my mother and heard the message of salvation. Eagerly, I gave my life to Christ and laid my weighty burdens upon Him. That night I found the answer to all of my fears and questions about eternity. And that night my physical healing began.

It was only when I stopped running, only when my heart reached back to Him, that my guilt vanished into peace and joy, and my depression ceased.

Jesus knew what resisting the fullness of fellowship with God could do to man. "It is hard to kick against the pricks," He told Saul (Acts 26:14). It is unnatural to live without God, and dangerous as well!

The Flip Side: Too Much Religion

But often Christians who have known the joy of forgiveness and fellowship with God find themselves slaves to a new kind of depression. The spiritual problem that causes depression more than anything else in Christians is an overdose of religion. It occurs gradually, when believers slip from their happy relationship with Jesus Christ into a bondage of church peer pressures, group convictions they do not share, and meaningless religious rituals and routines.

Unknowingly, they become strapped in a strait jacket of religiosity and legalism just as restrictive and meaningless as their previous habits and superstitions. Instead of enjoying the liberty of life in Christ, they turn to religious "forms" they can relate to, and interpret the convictions of others as their own. The life once shared with Jesus becomes crowded with repetitive prayers, church "busy work" without love and meaning, and other spiritual "disguises," which become a strangling yoke of bondage. Like a garden full of weeds, true life in Christ becomes choked by empty, hollow Christian service.

Don't misunderstand me! Christian service is our constant responsibility to God and the world. But unless our deeds are born in love, faith, and the Holy Spirit, that service means nothing to God, and only becomes a painted sepulcher for a dead relationship with Christ.

Unfortunately, I speak from experience. After several years in the ministry, I lost my joy and enthusiasm in the rush of every demanding day. Willing service soured into a sense of obligation, and my "ministry" seemed nothing more than any other job. No longer did I feel I knew what God wanted me to do in the press of circumstances, but more and more my decisions seemed based on the demands of people and religious form.

Then one day while driving home from the church, I broke down and cried. "God," I said, lifting my eyes skyward, "I love You, but I'm tired of living like this. I want to be me! I want to be free!"

As suddenly as I prayed, God spoke. "Bert, you are free," He said. "Be yourself. Bondage is not of Me."

It was then that I understood that I had so focused on the ministry that I had forgotten my source of strength and love. As I sought God in the following days, I lost my self-consciousness and found a new reservoir of fervent love.

The next Sunday, I preached with new power and conviction, and the people responded. That service was a watershed experience for the congregation. The church exploded with growth as the Lord blessed.

Religion can destroy you, but Jesus will set you free!

How well I remember one man in my flock who was a devoted, faithful member. Every service he sat in his customary place, and seldom failed to bring a friend.

But one Sunday evening, he visited another church and heard a minister warn about the dangers of a cultural evil—television. The man was impressed. He returned home and quickly sold his television set.

His convictions, however, didn't end with himself. He felt obligated to criticize others whose convictions did not conform to his own. Soon his critical spirit ostracized him from fellowship, and made him bitter. Finally, depressed, he came to my study for counseling. I showed him that truth is eternal and does not change with increasing technology. God gives convictions to every man, individually, to steer him away from the crags and rocks of life. And God reserves the right to convict others of His sheep. We don't have to do God's work for Him.

The man saw my point and accepted it. Today he is still serving Jesus with his old enthusiasm and faithfulness.

How can we shake ourselves free from religious forms? We must strive to keep standing firm and not be subjected again to a yoke of slavery (Galatans 5:1). We must accept our freedom in Christ, and understand that the broadness and completeness of His love transcends cultures to draw the entire world to Himself.

There is acceptance for everyone in that love. We can trust Him to guide us, to place the easy yoke of His authority upon us, to convict us personally of sin and habits that distract us from service unto Him, without adopting the convictions meant for others as our own.

As we love Him, we will be changed into His likeness. Often we cannot see that change occurring in us, but others see it, just as we see Christ at work in them. We learn from Him, and His character and love are reproduced in us. The fruit of the Spirit is not grown overnight, but it grows nonetheless—not because we have been chained to religious habits and empty phrases, but because His Spirit is within us, molding us and shaping us into His perfect image.

It is a *relationship* with Jesus that changes us, not religiosity. And through that relationship, depression and slavery are set aside for a life that is free indeed!

CHAPTER THREE

DISAPPOINTMENT AND REJECTION

If in your search for the causes of depression you conclude you have no physical problem, and you are in right standing with God, it's time to look outside the body. The pressures of modern life can converge on a person's emotions and spirit like deadly pincers—pressures which, when coupled with an intense emotional experience or disappointment, can topple emotional stability like a house of cards.

Few people become depresssed when things are going their way. But all too frequently, under pressure, even seemingly insignificant disappointment or personal loss can trigger it. Individuals who had once been buoyant, happy and fulfilled have been known to suffer depression from the loss of a family pet or from a child who didn't perform well at school. Normally, these are situations they could cope with; yet, because of other circumstances, these minor experiences become obstacles out of proportion in life and push them over the brink.

Never underestimate the proverbial molehill to a depressed person!

The most common source of disappointment which causes depression is disappointment in people. Too often those whom we admire and respect the most hurt us the most. Deliberately or unknowingly, they can betray our confidence, deceive us, trick us or belittle us. It is understandable that no one can walk through life without being hurt by other people. Although by faith we are being transformed into the image of Christ, we are not perfect. And we can hurt one another at times whether we mean to or not.

It makes sense that as long as we live in the world we will have occasion to deal with bitter disappointment. Don't be like the friend who once told me the only trusted companion he had in the world was his horse.

Depression, of course, doesn't come from people. Rather, it comes from what we do with our disappointment. If we nurse it instead of trying to understand and forgive it in ourselves and others, we will harbor it, and inside the spirit it will breed resentment or depression. To dwell on the failures of others is to dwell defeated.

It is important to make positive, inspirational thoughts our goal. "Whatever is true," the apostle Paul wrote, "whatever is honorable, whatever is right, whatever is pure, whatever is lovely, whatever is of good repute, if there is any excellence and if anything worthy of praise, let your mind dwell on these things" (Philippians 4:8).

Yet, while disappointment in people is a chief source of depression, disappointment in people *we love* is more damaging still. At one time or another, we expect to be the brunt of gossip from our co-workers on the office grapevine, or mistreated by a service station attendant or department store clerk. We expect to be treated rudely and insensitively by those we know only casually. It happens so often, in fact, that we approach our dealings with others with a curtain of steel drawn around our tender emotions.

But let a family member, a fellow church member, or close golfing buddy betray us or treat us indifferently, and the wounds dig deeper. Sometimes the slightest oversight can cause a family feud that lasts for years because that oversight, even unintentional, cuts to the quick of pride. That wall of steel simply wasn't made to keep out everyone, because we are creatures who need love, acceptance and companionship, even at the expense of great pain.

I know a man who is an example of that. After suffering through a painful divorce, he would sit quietly in his special chair, looking blankly into space. He had been hurt by the one he loved the most and suspected the least, and he rejected the world because of it. He shut himself off because he failed to deal with the disappointment and agony he felt inside.

Like this man, we all need to be loved, faults and all, yet we recoil at the feeling of rejection we experience when someone inside that inner curtain reacts to a fault in us.

We hurt because the rejection is unexpected. Mentally we rationalize that those who don't know us well can't appreciate us, while those who do know us should. We fail to see that those who know us best also know and tolerate our personal failures even more acutely than others, yet from these we expect love, respect, security and unconditional acceptance.

We put great demands on those who love us! Remember that the next time someone fails you!

In all my years of ministry, I've never met a perfect individual. I've never met a person who was lovable in all phases of his character, personality and physical attractiveness. But I've never met anyone who could live without love, either. All of us need love, and all of us look to others for that love and respect. Surely we must often close our eyes to the imperfections of people in order to love them, but we must also realize that they sometimes overlook our faults to love us.

To put the Golden Rule a different way: "Love others in spite of their failures, even as you would have others love you in spite of yours." Love the whole person for who he is—for Whose he is—and for what he means to God.

Because we have inadequacies in our ability to love, many people walk through life empty. There are no vacancy signs pinned to their lapels, but their lives are empty of love. They are lonely, and they fail to know how to change that fact. It is the empty, lonely people who suffer depression easiest, for with no love to comfort them—with no one to reach out to —they turn inward. Once the spirit is hopeless and ceases to search and reach for love, it begins to die. Humans are like trees in that respect: Trees that stop reaching stop growing, and then they die.

The Advantage of Faith

People who believe and trust in God have many advantages over non-believers in obtaining victory over depression. Their first step to freedom comes from their relationship with Jesus Christ. "If therefore the Son shall make you free, you shall be free indeed" (John 8:36). They are also surrounded by a family of other believers at church who are concerned for them, who can express faith through prayer and action. Friends of like faith are a positive force to lean upon in times of crises. The support of a Christian family and church body can save your life.

Christian friends are even a great comfort in death.

Earl Dial was a faithful, beloved member of a church I pastored in LaGrande, Oregon. He was as Christ-like as any man I've ever known, and he was a victim of terminal cancer.

I remember the night Earl was promoted to heaven. I sat in his hospital room with his wife, his son and other family members. We were calm and peaceful because we knew that Earl, though now unconscious, had never been afraid to die.

In the early morning hours, those of us who huddled around the bedside became aware of God's presence, like a fragrance, filling the room. I turned to Earl's wife and said, "God's Spirit is so near. It must be that time for Earl." We turned toward him, just in time to see him breathe his last in this life and fall into the Lord's peaceful sleep.

Believe me when I tell you: There are definite advantages to serving God.

The attitude of faith itself can combat depression. Faith is the calm assurance we have of God's providence and provision. It is the inclination of our hearts toward Him: always upward, always trusting, always knowing that His will is best for us. It is the attitude that guarded and guided Earl.

Even when a suffering individual lacks that faith because of a desperate situation, the congregation of God's people should be full of it.

Christians express their faith by faithfulness to God's house. Sermons are not always inspiring and activities are not always meaningful, but

God's people are faithful to Him by not failing to assemble together.

The word "faithful," after all, means "full of faith." Hearts that are full of faith are those who look beyond external conditions to see God's ability to create and love and heal. People who are full of faith are secure in God, and can reach outwardly to share their bountiful blessings with others.

Christians with faith are blessings indeed to those in depression.

The Therapy of Forgiveness

How can one who has been injured by his disappointment in another person rebound into right relationship with God and men? Try expressing the faith you already possess: *forgive!* It takes faith and assurance in God's love to forgive, and it can work the deepest healing in a human heart.

One school teacher told me that he had never been depressed until his wife suddenly divorced him and married another man. He had been so busy with his work, caring for others, that he had neglected the one person most valuable to him—his wife. The loss tore his heart out, and he was depressed for an entire year.

He was depressed until he learned to forgive. He learned to forgive those who had wronged him. He even forgave himself.

Perhaps something similar has happened to

you. For a little while bleed inside, if you have to; hurt if you must. Cry the night away, but don't blame others. Ask for God's grace and guidance. He is always sufficient.

Here's a promise we can hold close: "But we have this treasure in earthen vessels, that the surpassing greatness of the power may be of God and not from ourselves; we are afflicted in every way, but not crushed; perplexed, but not despairing; persecuted, but not forsaken; struck down, but not destroyed. . . .For momentary, light affliction is producing for us an eternal weight of glory far beyond all comparison, while we look not at the things which are seen, but at the things which are not seen; for the things which are seen are temporal, but the things which are not seen are eternal" (2 Corinthians 4:7-9,17-18).

Great promise, isn't it?

CHAPTER FOUR

THE DANGERS OF SELF-HATE

Hardly anyone who is depressed loves himself. By its nature, depression brings self-doubt, insecurity, guilt and condemnation, which in time can destroy an individual's healthy sense of self-worth. For that reason, counselors and ministers frequently try to combat depression by building up a person's confidence and self-esteem. In the overwhelming number of cases, patients who improve the evaluation they have of themselves also shed their depression.

There are numerous reasons why a person can lose respect for himself. Perhaps he began with a poor self-opinion through an association with a religion of debasement and condemnation. Too many religious groups—and misguided individuals—try to relate to God by purifying their bodies through rituals and determined abstinence from all earthly pleasures, as if such "purification" can justify them before God.

Self-punishment has been practiced by sincerely

religious men and women for centuries. This was true of Martin Luther, the founder of Protestantism, before he recognized the important truth of justification by faith. Luther, to be sure, was earnest in his self-debasement. He began his career as a German monk hoping to compensate for his sins through the renunciation of self-will, a scant diet, rough clothing, vigils by night and labors by day, mortification of the flesh, poverty, and begging.

He prayed seven times a day, including nightly sessions in the chapel at two o'clock in the morning. When he slept, he put away blankets to suffer through the wintry German nights.

So intent was his striving for purity that Luther later wrote, "I was a good monk, and I kept the rule of my order so strictly the I may say that if ever a monk got to heaven by his monkery, it was I. All my brothers in the monastery who knew me will bear me out. If I had kept on any longer, I should have killed myself with vigils, prayers, reading, and other work."

But did physical abuse bring peace with God? No, Luther said. Rather, it confirmed all the more that man cannot reach his Creator through his own clumsy efforts.

Sadly, so may innocent, searching people continue to try Luther's first path to God. Yet though they adhere to strict forms of behavior and deny themselves of physical comforts, they remain troubled. Even with complete devotion to their quest for God, they hear a constant, probing accusation that comes straight from Satan himself. "But have you fasted *enough*?" he will say. Or, "Have you prayed *enough*? Are your motives pure *enough*? Pray more! Fast more! It's impossible to be *good enough* for God!"

And, of course, he is right. Christianity was never intended to be lived by rules and rituals. Jesus never intended it to be a system of self-inflicted punishment, for our efforts alone can never merit the salvation of God. "For by grace you have been saved through faith; and that not of yourselves, it is the gift of God," Paul wrote, "not as a result of works, that no one should boast" (Ephesians 2:8, 9). Jesus intended us to live in free and open relationship with Him, "for we do not have a high priest who cannot sympathize with our weaknesses, but one who has been tempted in all things as we are, yet without sin" (Hebrews 4:15).

Read this important statement from Colossians 2:8-10, 18-23:

"See to it that no one takes you captive through philosophy and empty deception, according to the tradition of men, according to the elementary principles of the world, rather than according to Christ. For in Him all the fullness of Deity dwells in bodily form, and in Him you have been made complete.

"Let no one keep defrauding you of your prize *by <u>delighting in self-debasement</u> a*nd the worship of the angels, taking his stand on visions he has seen, inflated without cause by his fleshly mind, and not holding fast to the head, from whom the entire body, being supplied and held together by the joints and ligaments, grows with a growth which is from God.

"If you have died with Christ to the elementary principles of the world, why, as if you were living in the world, do you submit yourselves to decrees, such as, *'Do not handle, do not taste, do not touch!'* (which all refer to things destined to perish with the using)—in accordance with the commandments and teachings of men? These are matters which have, to be sure, the appearance of wisdom in self-made religion and self-abasement and servere treatment of the body, *but are of no value against fleshly indulgence."*

God Does Not Accuse

Most people who practice such forms of physical abasement do so to score points with God. But their actions point out a dangerous misunderstanding of God's Word, or a spiritual insecurity in God's provision in salvation.

What must we do to merit God's grace? Someone once asked that question in Jesus' day. "What shall we do, that we may work the works of God?" said a voice in the multitude. Christ's answer was simple and direct: "This is the work of God, that you believe in Him whom He has sent" (John 6:28-29). The whole of our relationship with Him comes by faith.

During periods when we feel the most unworthy and condemned, we must remember where that feeling comes from. We must remember where accusations come from! It was Satan who accused Job before God, and it is Satan who accuses today. He lays condemnation where no condemnation belongs. "There is now no condemnation for those who are in Christ Jesus" (Romans 8:1), yet Satan tries to make us apologize for being born. Rather than fulfilling our God-granted potential, Satan pounds our minds with memories of past failures. If we continually believe him, he would cause us to see ourselves as creatures totally without beauty and value. Yet we know we have worth before God, for "while we were yet sinners, Christ died for us" (Romans 5:8).

What kind of husband are you? Satan will say you are harsh and miserly, even though you work hard to make a living and provide for your family.

What kind of wife are you? Satan will tell you the years of physical beauty have passed you by. Is it wrong to grow older? A grandmother with a wrinkled face and a tired body is beautiful in God's eyes and in the eyes of a loving husband. Her beauty is spiritual and moral, deeper than carnal attractiveness. Through the years, that grandmother has brought life into the world, nursed sickness and taught the love of Christ by word and example. She is lovely! Though the freshness of youth fades for all of us, it is replaced with a maturity of experience and character that only time can produce. That grandmother becomes the pride of her husband, the joy of her children. She shouldn't feel depressed for growing older. She should feel wonderful!

The loss of self-esteem and worth comes by believing the worst about yourself, told by Satan, the father of lies (John 8:44). God has made us unique individuals in Him, full of promising talents and abilities. We must learn to see ourselves as God sees us! We must learn we are lovely in Christ!

CHAPTER FIVE

THE DANGERS OF UNFAIR COMPARISON

It's really no wonder that so many millions suffer from depression these days. Every waking moment we are bombarded by subtle messages that appeal to our selfish tendencies and desires. We are told we can look younger and more appealing through our association with toothpastes, hair colors, double-knit suits and sleek sports cars. The pressure is overpowering in our society to be sexy, athletic, outgoing and young.

Let's face it: Not all of us are attractive. And everyone who lives long enough will lose his youth. In a society that rewards such carnal characteristics, all of us will sooner or later face a crisis in confidence. To some of us, that crisis will tunnel into depression.

It may come through balding, turning forty, or losing teeth, but it will come. How can we minimize the effects of such realities?

First of all, it is necessary for all of us to know ourselves, with our strengths and weaknesses.

fairly "sized up." Some men and women are organizers, while some work better "off the cuff." Some accomplish more under pressure, while others like tranquil surroundings. Many people are physically tough enough to continue with only a few hours of sleep each night, while others are more fragile, and require ample rest. Learning comes easily to some, while others must study diligently.

It is personal characteristics such as these that make us truly individual, and we must understand them within ourselves. More importantly, we must accept them in ourselves and cultivate them into advantages.

To be the best we can be we must know ourselves as Jesus knows us. We can ask the Lord, as David did, to examine our hearts, eliminating the bad and bringing out the good (Psalm 139:23-24). We must also like the person that we are. In order to love your neighbor as yourself, you must first acknowledge that you are a unique individual in Jesus Christ and that you love the person He has made you! This healthy respect of self is a cornerstone to happiness and mental stability throughout life.

But when individuals have little or no understanding of their uniqueness, too often they desire the talents and strengths of others. Many a young man has visualized himself a football hero, and many a young girl has envied the pretty blond senior who is crowned prom sweetheart. We like the qualities and abilities of other people and wish they were ours. So we daydream. We fantasize. No harm done, right?

Perhaps, until that longing to be something other than what we are ceases to be inspiration and becomes frustration. Then, those "harmless" comparisons with others can lead to depression.

Paul said, "For we are not bold to class or compare ourselves with some of those who commend themselves; but when they measure themselves by themselves, and compare themselves with themselves, they are without understanding" (2 Corinthians 10:12).

Most often the comparisons we make—when we stack our "chips" alongside someone else's pile—are unfair. Matching an area of our deficiency against another person's strength is certainly unfair.

Consider, for example, the woman who is known internationally for her glamour and good looks. Beauty is her strong suit, and she works hard at it. She conditions her body with exercise, medication, sleep and proper meals. She hires beauty experts to advise her. Take away her beauty, and you would probably take away her international reputation and, furthermore, her self-identity.

How wise is any woman, attractive but gifted in some other area, who compares herself to such an acclaimed beauty?

Or consider the plant foreman who has ambitions of writing—who writes in captured moments after work each night. How can he fairly compare himself to the playwright who has studied his craft and has devoted an entire life to it?

Likewise, material comparisons are unfair and unwise. Self-esteem cannot be measured by a brick mansion with a swimming pool and manicured yard. Possessions may be convenient and may impress our friends, but they also exact a price. Have you ever considered how much money and effort it takes to support and maintain such a luxurious estate? It can become such a snare, until we become captives of the things we possess, until we spend more time maintaining and supporting them than enjoying them. If you doubt that, I have some personal research for you. Through the years, dozens of wealthy people have complained to me about the emptiness of possessions. Some of the wealthiest people in the world would gladly trade their riches for peace and simplicity.

Kind David, himself a prosperous man, wrote, "For I was envious of the arrogant, as I saw the prosperity of the wicked." Result? "My feet came close to stumbling; my steps had almost slipped," (Psalm 73:2).

Our example to live by comes from Hebrews 13:5-6, which exhorts: "Let your way of life be free from the love of money, being content with what you have; for He Himself has said, 'I will never desert you, nor will I ever forsake you,' so that we confidently say, 'The Lord is my helper, I will not be afraid. What shall man do to me?' "

The secret is to be content with what we are, with what we have, and with what we can expect. It takes faith in God to be content. We must find our existence in Him, and realize He has a purpose for us wherever He has placed us in life and in His Body (1 Corinthians 12:18).

Different people have different gifts and talents. None of us is without them. Our responsibility is to find our greatest areas of strength and utilize them fully.

Jesus once told the parable of three servants who worked for an extremely wealthy man. To the most promising employee, the rich man committed five talents; The second servant received three talents; the third received one. Each received, Jesus said, according to his own ability.

Certainly the wealthy patron realized the abilities of his servants. It would have been foolish to entrust five talents to the least capable servant, and unfair to give a single talent to the most promising man.

Moreover, it would have been extremely damaging for the one talent servant to compare his position with the man of five talents. Perhaps the most honored man was older, more experienced, more disciplined and knowledgeable. Or perhaps the one talent servant was a brilliant farmer, but knew little of investments. We aren't told. We are only exhorted, like the servants, to do the best we have with what we're given, being mindful that all we have has been entrusted to us. "From everyone who has been given much shall much be required;" "Jesus said, "and to whom they entrusted much, of him they will ask all the more" (Luke 12:48).

Becoming the Most

Occasionally a one talent man will accomplish more than a five talent man simply because he applies himself more. Oh, he may or may not finish with the pile of goods that the wealthier man has, but because of a humble start, he may actually cover more ground. What honor has a sprinter who never trains and never wins?

Don't compare! Participate! Play the game of life contented and confident in the measure of ability God has given you. Remember, God gives the gifts as He sees fit.

As a young man, I accepted the pastorship in a church that had been guided by the same man for twenty-seven years. My predecessor was a unique and much-loved man. Because of my earnest desire to serve and please, and because of my feelings of inadequacy, I tried in every way to be exactly like that respected minister. He wore a tie when he went hunting, so I did. He always wore a hat, so I tried it.

Of course, my hat and tie made me no better a person or minister. One day I realized that God had created me a unique individual, different to be sure, but just as important. I learned to relax in God and be myself.

Another time, still in my younger days, I attended a convention where a respected and beloved pastor gave the keynote address. I was greatly impressed and moved by both the sermon and the man of God, and I looked for ways to approach him. But every time I moved towards him, he stepped away as though he was purposely ignoring me. For a young minister trying to find acceptance and respect among peers, his slight was a painful blow.

"So that's it," I finally told myself. "He thinks he's better than me. Why is it that when so many men make it to the top of the ladder, they forget what it's like below?"

Immediately, I felt bad about my attitude. I left the sanctuary in an attempt to gain control of my feelings.

Actually, I felt sorry for myself, but not enough to repent of my feelings. When I stepped back inside the sanctuary, I immediately spotted the respected pastor, now standing all alone.

"Well, this is it," I said self-righteously. "I'll be a Christian even if he isn't." And I approached him.

This time he couldn't avoid me. When I drew

near, I summoned my most spiritual sounding voice and said, "Sir, that was a great message. I want you to know how much I love and respect you."

I'll never forget the force of his deep eyes upon me, as if peering through me into my heart. He smiled, then said meekly, "Thank you, young man. Now, what is your name?"

You see, I felt inferior and thought that great man of God didn't like me when, in reality, he didn't even know me. Oh, the sin of unfair comparisons.

The tragedy of comparing ourselves to others is that God desired to make us each differently so that He might reveal Himself to His Body and to the world in a million individual ways. To be like others is to limit God in our lives.

Avoid a tragedy. Learn to find the loveliness of being yourself.

CHAPTER SIX

SIN OR SICKNESS

Because of growing pressure within American society, depression has reached epidemic proportions. Research shows that one of every eight individuals will experience it so acutely this year that they will seek outside help. That means almost eight million boys, girls, men and women of all ages, social groups and economic classifications will become so devastated by its effects that they will turn to professionals for answers. Millions of others will suffer silently. And because depression unchecked is a stepping stone to suicide, suicide will rank again this year as the fifth largest killer in America, nearly as indiscriminate and deadly as heart disease or cancer.

Certainly there is a troubling paradox surrounding depression. Its effects upon the human body and mind parallel the effects of other debilitating diseases. We have seen how depression causes a loss of appetite and, consequently, a loss of weight, a loss of concentration and sexual drive, while creating a dangerous susceptibility to other illnesses.

But perhaps the most harmful results of depression are spiritual ones. Depression causes normally out-going personalities to lock themselves into seclusion, to question self-worth and ability, to suspect the intents and motives of others who would be otherwise trusted. It brings indecision, rejection, hurt, loneliness, frustration, despair, emptiness and isolation, while sapping vitality and joy.

Depression is sadness and constant fearfulness, much like sitting alone in a dark house, listening to every creaky, spooky sound.

With all its physical and spiritual consequences, how do we classify depression? Is it a sickness or a sin? To understand the answer to that important question, we must probe into the nature of depression itself.

A Crisis of Faith

First of all, while depression brings by nature a crisis of faith, the experience itself does not mean a loss of faith. To be sure, the prayers of a depressed Christian seem to hit a sky made of brass, and God seems a million miles away. Bible reading often becomes a hollow chore during depression, a far different experience than the lifegiving blessing it usually is.

But faith in God does not depend upon feelings. The faithful will still pray and cling to the provisions of God's Word, no matter what the surrounding conditions and circumstances.

King David knew such feelings. "Be gracious to me, O Lord," he wrote, "for I am pining away; heal me, O Lord, for my bones are dismayed. And my soul is greatly dismayed; but Thou, O Lord—how long?

"I am weary with my sighing; every night I make my bed swim, I dissolve my couch with my tears. My eye has wasted away with grief; it has become old because of all my adversaries."

Yet, despite his personal torment, David maintained his faith: "Depart from me, all you who do iniquity, for the Lord has heard the voice of my weeping. The Lord has heard my supplication, the Lord receives my prayer" (Psalm 6:8,9).

On another occasion he wrote, "Why dost Thou stand afar off, O Lord? Why dost Thou hide Thyself in times of trouble?" (Psalm 10:1).

The David who penned such words while in the throes of depression is the same man who also proclaimed the steadfastness of God! "O Lord, Thou hast heard the desire of the humble; Thou wilt strengthen their heart, Thou wilt incline Thine ear" (Psalm 10:17). "The Lord also will be a stronghold for the oppressed, a stronghold in times of trouble, and those who know Thy name will put their trust in Thee; for Thou, O Lord, have not forsaken those who seek Thee" (Psalm 9:9-10).

Surely the prophet Daniel understood how to pray when the heavens seemed closed to prayer. Troubled in spirit, he mourned three weeks for his people, Israel, praying continously without eating.

His diligence lasted the entire twenty-one days, when in a vision, he received the answer he sought. Had God failed to hear his prayers for three weeks? Hardly! The Bible quotes Daniel's angelic messenger: "Do not be afraid, Daniel, for from the first day that you set your heart on understanding this and on humbling yourself before your God, your words were heard, and I have come in response to your words" (Daniel 10:12).

If any man who has ever lived knew the depths of depression, it was Job. Because of his renowned faith in God, he became involved in an eternal struggle between his Creator and Satan, who wished to destroy him. With God's permission, Job lost his children, his wealth, his possessions, his friends and health. Yet, though depressed and scourged, pressed to the limit of man's endurance, he spoke words of eternal faith. Though it seemed he had been smitten by a harsh judge he could not see or cry to, Job said, "Behold, I go forward but He is not there, and backwards, but I cannot perceive Him; when he acts on the left, I cannot behold Him; He turns on the right, I cannot see Him.

"*But He knows the way I take;* when He has tried me, I shall come forth as gold. My foot has held fast to His path; I have kept His way and not turned aside. I have not departed from the command of His lips; I have treasured the words of His mouth more than my necessary food. It is God who has made my heart faint, and the Almighty who has dismayed me, but I am not silenced by the darkness, nor deep gloom which covers me" (Job 23:10-12,16,17).

Job, like Daniel and David, understood that depression was only a tool for spiritual growth, when seen from God's perspective.

For that reason, I am convinced that depression is not a sin. The storms and winds and poundings of life are ordained for every man. These are not sin. Sin, rather, is determined by our response to these problems.

We know, for example, that every man who lives is tempted to sin. Jesus, who committed no sin, was tempted. But temptation itself is not sin. It remains our choice how to respond to that temptation. "But each one is tempted when he is carried away and enticed by his own lust. Then when lust has conceived, it gives birth to sin; and when sin is accomplished, it brings forth death" (James 1:14-15).

Consider anger. Usually we don't classify anger

as an acceptable Christian response to a problem of life. James 1:19 says, "But let everyone be quick to hear, slow to speak and slow to anger." Yet anger itself is not sin. Jesus was angry on several occasions, and Paul exhorted, "Be angry, and yet do not sin; do not let the sun go down on your anger" (Ephesians 4:26).

No, depression, like temptation and anger, is not a sin. True, sin can find place inside a troubled heart more readily than inside a buoyant one, but the experience itself is no transgression against God. It is when we remain in our depression and refuse to be comforted that depression can become sin.

What is depression? It is heart sickness, an infirmity in the spirit of man. As such, it can be healed by Him who has a nature to heal. Jesus can heal completely in body, mind and spirit. "Heal my soul," David wrote in Psalm 41:4. The healing of Christ can accomplish it.

Rarely have I met a depressed person who wanted to be depressed. But it affects everyone, without discrimination and without exception, at one time or another. We must learn to conquer it. We must learn to grow from it.

We must learn to call upon Him who sets at liberty those who are captive. He can restore us, lift us and heal us from all our hurts, even the hurts of our hearts.

CHAPTER SEVEN

ELIJAH'S DEPRESSION

We heap a great burden of affection on the men and women of the ministry. The more success and effectiveness our pastors and evangelists enjoy, the more we revere them. Through them, we hope to find Jesus, so we study their words and lifestyles and mimic their mannerisms.

Yet there is nothing about the ministry that makes the minister any less human than a layman. In fact, too often ministers are just as failure-prone as their congregations. We are wise to remember that the only difference between the minister and his flock is the calling upon him!

The Bible is full of spiritual heroes for us to glean from, yet every one of them was as human and fallible as we are. Elijah, the great Old Testament prophet, is certainly an outstanding example of one who was intimate with the mind and power of God, yet the Scriptures deliberately tell us that "he was a man with a nature like ours" (James 5:17).

If our nature includes periodic discouragement and depression, then Elijah is indeed an outstanding example!

The Ravings of Jezebel — Background

Elijah was an unusual man in several respects. Before he stepped onto the national scene in Israel (1 Kings 17), we have no mention of him. He was an obscure Tishbite dressed in unorthodox clothes who boldly approached King Ahab one day and said, "as the Lord, the God of Israel lives, before whom I stand, surely there shall be neither dew nor rain these years, except by my word."

Regardless of anything else we might think about Elijah, we must consider him a courageous man! No coward would dare approach the king of Israel with such a reckless statement!

We know now, of course, that Elijah was also a man of exceptional faith. James 5:17 says he was a man with a nature like ours, who "prayed earnestly that it might not rain." Elijah had found the mind of God, had prayed in accordance with the will of God, and, convinced of his authority and right convictions, had dared challenge a king.

Three years passed by, without a drop of rain. By the second time Elijah approached Ahab, he was a fugitive with a price on his head. Ahab wanted him dead or alive. But God was with Elijah, and the prophet arranged a dramatic confrontation between the prophet of God and the prophets of Baal at Mount Carmel. The winner would represent the living God of Israel; the loser would be killed.

According to Scripture, Elijah's God did what the prayers of 450 prophets of Baal could not do. Following a simple prayer from Elijah, the God of heaven swept down upon a water-drenched sacrifice and devoured it with fire. Thus, Elijah was vindicated, the prophets of Baal slain, and God proven anew to the house of Israel. It was perhaps Elijah's greatest hour. That dry afternoon, after bringing such a complete victory for his God, Elijah prayed again, and it rained heavily.

A hero of faith? Exactly. But notice how quickly that spiritual giant became human again! Here's what we read in 1 Kings 19:1-3:

"Now Ahab told Jezebel all that Elijah had done, and how he had killed all the prophets with the sword. Then Jezebel sent a messenger to Elijah, saying, 'So may the gods do to me and even more, if I do not make your life as the life of one of them by tomorrow about this time.' And he was afraid and arose and ran for his life and came to Beersheba, which belongs to Judah, and left his servant there."

Suddenly, in a startling reversal, the man of faith became a man of fear. Elijah became discouraged.

But why? He had stood three years with his God. He had prayed for Israel. He had camped beside the brook Cherith until the drought dried up all the mountain streams. He had been fed miraculously by ravens, and had even raised a widow's son from the dead. Alone, he had faced Ahab, the prophets of Baal, and all Israel. He had won victories no other human being could claim. Why was this tremendous man of faith now troubled by the threats of evil Jezebel?

I believe Elijah became frightened by Jezebel because he did not expect adversity in the pursuit of God's will. Elijah had grown confident as he walked in the power of God. But here, for the first time, came resistance, and Elijah was unprepared.

There is an important lesson to learn from Elijah's encounter with Jezebel. As long as we walk with God, winning battles of faith in His name, as long as we pray and move forward in His authority, we are going to face opposition. We must expect it, and we must prepare for it. As soon as we announce we are going to preach the gospel, our lives may begin to fall apart. Friends and family members will tell us we're crazy to leave a cozy job for a ministry that promises us nothing. Satan will see to it that the car continuously needs repair, that the furnace breaks down, the air conditioner burns out, or the roof leaks. In a thousand ways, as we step out for God, we will find every excuse to turn tail and run.

Some of those excuses will come from within us. Inside our heart, we will find doubts about our ability and fears about the surrounding circumstances. Left alone, those doubts and fears can choke out the command of God for our lives and our response of faith. We must not cower before opposition. We must fight it through prayer and realize that God never called a man who could finish the course without Him.

Perhaps Elijah felt Jezebel's threats meant God had abandoned him. After all, God had told him about Ahab and the prophets of Baal. But God *didn't* tell him about Jezebel!

At this point, I am reminded how Christ's disciples must have felt after an exhausting day of ministry in the hot Palestine sun. When Jesus finished teaching the multitudes, he pointed to a boat tied to the shore of the Sea of Galilee.

"There," He said, "let's get in the boat and go to the other side."

Once aboard, the Master laid down and quickly fell asleep.

It wasn't long before the bright sky became black and the placid sea turned stormy. The winds thundered down the slopes of the Galilean hills and turned the sea into a tumultuous, crashing storm. Many of the disciples had long been fishermen and had seen these sudden squalls before, but this was no ordinary storm! The wooden planks creaked with the strain and the deck groaned against the pounding surf. Even to these veteran seamen, the boat was nearly lost! In panic, they awakened their sleeping Master.

"Save us, Lord; for we are perishing!" one said.

Then Jesus made a remarkable comment. Before rebuking the winds and sea—even before rising from His bed—He scolded His chosen companions.

"Why are you timid, you men of little faith?" He asked.

Little faith? Weren't these the twelve who had watched daily as Jesus performed countless miracles throughout Israel? They had lived with Him, supped with Him. Why, they were on board that creaking, floundering vessel in the first place only at His request. Was it so wrong to turn in desperation to the only one who could save them?

Jesus, however, knew the fear that was in their hearts and knew they didn't understand the promise hidden in every command of God. Before ever leaving shore, He had instructed His friends to depart to the other side. When the Master instructs us to proceed to the oppostite shore, what storm, no matter how furious, can prevent our safe arrival? The promise of every command is that He will never give us more than we can bear, that He will never order us to do what He is unwilling to help us with, and that we will never have to go alone.

We have a promise to back up the command. So why do we sometimes assume our obedience will go unopposed or untested? The steps of faith will know opposition. We must understand it and be prepared.

Sadly for Elijah, however, he listened to Jezebel's threat. He forgot the provisions afforded by the call of God, and he ran.

Before heaping condemnation on Elijah, let us remember who this was who ran from the threats of Jezebel. Elijah was the man mightily used of God. The only difference between the Elijah of Mount Carmel and the Elijah of Beersheba was discouragement.

The next time you are discouraged, remember: Battles are never won while retreating. Problems don't fade away because we run from them.

Discouragement is the spiritual condition that presents itself when we cringe before circumstances and question the ability of God. Suddenly, Elijah's faith melted. He lost confidence. He questioned his mission and calling.

More importantly, Elijah found that discouragement causes loss of memory. Had he stopped long enough, he surely would have remembered the powerful deeds of God over the previous three years. Confidence is built on past experiences! Trust grows because our confidence in Christ grows from spiritual triumph to spiritual triumph. Had Elijah paused to pray, he surely would have said, "The God who delivered me from Ahab will certainly keep me from Ahab's wife."

But discouragement, and the self-doubt and fear that accompany it, cannot remember the wonders that God performs routinely for His children.

The faith that responds to God would have us scatter our fear. Instead of being awed by visible circumstances, our spiritual eyes must keep steady gaze on Christ. In Deuteronomy 1:28, God reminded the people of Israel that fear had kept them from the land He had promised them. "Where can we go up?" the people had said. "Our brethern have made our hearts melt, saying, 'The people are bigger and taller than we; the cities are large and fortified to heaven.' "

Yet God said to them, "Do not be shocked, nor fear them. The Lord your God who goes before you will Himself fight on your behalf, just as He did for you in Egypt before your eyes."

Cast down fear! Remember the faithfulness of God!

Elijah's unresolved discouragement led him into the depths of depression. 1 Kings 19:4 explains that "he himself went a day's journey into the wilderness, and came and sat down under a juniper tree; and requested for himself that he might die, and said, 'It is enough; now, O Lord, take my life, for I am not better than my fathers.' "

Elijah asked to die, but did he really mean what he prayed? No. It would have been just as easy to be killed by Jezebel's henchmen in the city than collapse and die in the wilderness. The prophet didn't want to die, but in his depression, he felt as if he did. That feeling is the dangerous difference between discouragement and depression. Discouragement makes you feel the you don't want to continue the battle. Depression makes you feel you *can't*.

Thankfully, God understands depression. He knows our momentary loss of inner balance will cause us to say things we otherwise don't mean. God understood Elijah's prayer as a cry from the depths of his hurting soul. And God was faithful. He sent an angel to feed and encourage His servant.

I, too, have voiced my despair in prayers to God. How grateful I am that He understood my pit of depression and cared for me. I'm glad He overlooked the words that poured from my mouth and saw deeper into my heart.

God heard the prayers of Elijah and sent help. He dealt with His prophet under a juniper tree and restored Elijah's soul! He can do the same today!

There are two lessons to learn from the story of Elijah. First, we know that if a man of Elijah's spiritual stature can suffer discouragement and depression, then every one of us can. And will. Secondly, we learn that God understands the crying of an anguished heart and is faithful to meet us in our moment of need, even under a juniper tree.

And then, we can also discover the lesson that Christ's disciples found so true: that if the Master of heaven asks us to sail with Him across life, we can enjoy the journey. For what struggle of life and heart can hinder our safe arrival?

CHAPTER EIGHT

JONAH'S PIT

If you've never been known to let your responsibility slide a little while you take a holiday of your own, let me introduce you to someone who did. Jonah was a prophet of ancient Israel who became so renowned for running from responsibility that we've coined a term for others just like him. Perhaps you've known a self-willed "Jonah" in your city or on your job.

Jonah's story is important because he, like Elijah, was closely acquainted with God. He knew the voice of God, and knew he had a unique calling and purpose.

And, like Elijah, Jonah was a man on the run, a man whose running took him to the depths of depression and despair, yet for vastly different reasons. Elijah ran from fear and self-doubt caused by Satan's opposition after he had obeyed the commandment of God. But Jonah ran from the outset. Jonah ran from the commandment itself.

How To Choose A Prophet

Let the Bible pick up the story:

"The word of the Lord came to Jonah, the son of Amittai saying, 'Arise, go to Nineveh the great city and cry against it, for their wickedness has come up before Me.' But Jonah rose up to flee from the presence of the Lord. So he went down to Joppa, found a ship which was going to Tarshish, paid the fare, and went down into it to go with them to Tarshish from the presence of the Lord" (Jonah 1:1-3).

It is easier to understand why Jonah chose to flee from God when we first understand the commandment God gave him. Nineveh, you see, was a Gentile city. Its reputation in Israel during Jonah's lifetime was one of debauchery, adultery and idol worship. Nineveh's 120,000 residents had no fear for the God of Israel or His laws. Their society was carnal, materialistic and violent. In Jonah's vernacular, Ninevehites were heathen.

So God's commandment came as a jolting blow to Jonah. After all, Jonah was an Israelite, a chosen prophet of a chosen people, who had been raised in the traditions of Moses. He knew the Torah as well as he knew the Palestine hills, for he had long devoted himself to study. He, like every other Israelite, knew the provisions of Jehovah's law, how providential blessing would cover the land as long as God's people honored His law and walked in His statutes. The law pervaded all of

Jonah's life, laying down God's judgment upon idol worship, adultery and other wrongdoing so common in Nineveh. For such sins, Israel had often been punished. In fact, Jonah may have thought that Israel had been punished for transgressions far smaller than those committed daily in wicked Nineveh!

But Jonah also understood the mercy of God. His law provided for hungry strangers who sojourned in Israel, and treated orphans and widows kindly. Jonah was as acquainted with God's compassion as he was with God's unswerving justice. Jonah said to God, "For I knew that Thou art a gracious and compassionate God, slow to anger and abundant in loving kindness, and one who relents concerning calamity" (Jonah 4:2).

So, Jonah wondered, why would God call a prophet from Israel to a wicked city like Nineveh unless He intended to allow the city to repent (Jonah 4:2)?

The thought of Nineveh's repentance chilled Jonah. It was unacceptable! Better for God to destroy the city's evil inhabitants in a demonstration of justice than accept repentance, he thought.

Jonah's attitude, of course, was colored by prejudicial training and background. His reaction was much like ours when we are asked to show some kindness to someone we don't like or don't know. Our conditioning makes us cringe. Jonah thought God was surely mistaken. Nobody deserved punishment any more than did the Ninevehites!

So Jonah made up his mind. Since God was making a grave mistake sending a preacher to such a wicked city, Jonah would see to it that the preacher never arrived!

We may chuckle at Jonah's decision, but his plight is a universal one. At one time or other, all of us have tried to tell God how to tend His business. Jonah couldn't understand God's reasoning. He couldn't accept God's commandment, and he wasn't about to obey. He rebelled because he didn't want to do what God wanted to have done.

Instead, he decided to buy a ticket to a city at the opposite end of the world. As far as he was concerned, he was finished as a prophet. "Forget the ministry!" Jonah may have said. Let God find someone else to preach to that Gentile city. It was no concern of his.

At this point, we might rightly ask why God called Jonah for this task in the first place. He was self-willed, prejudiced and arrogant. Who could use a man like that?

Fortunately, God could! God has reasons for calling men and women that are unexplainable to us. Jesus, for example, chose impulsive Simon Peter to become a member of his inner circle of disciples. God called Gideon to lead armies when he was so afraid of the Philistines that he ground his wheat in a wine press where no one was looking. God chose stiff-necked, compromising Sampson, who fought more battles with himself than he ever did against the enemy, and weak Baalam, a man who delivered God's message with such reluctance that God once had to open the mouth of Baalam's donkey to chasten him.

Thankfully, for reasons He alone knows, God called you and me, not for what we are, but for what He has the power to make us. He asks us to give Him our humble talents, then He molds us to reach our highest potential.

I am blessed to have a son who followed me into the ministry. David has written books and touched the lives of thousands. But David wasn't always an evangelist. I remember holding him in my arms when he was but a few minutes old, and I watched him grow and develop through the years.

Did I realize then what effectiveness my son would someday have for God? No! I held in my arms a helpless, tiny baby boy, unable to speak, walk or feed himself. He was totally unable to sustain himself.

That is where we were when God chose us. We were helpless, totally reliant upon Him. But God knows our end from our beginning. He called us to develop us into men and women who can accomplish exploits for Him.

The God who sees the future is a merciful God! He knows every stumble and mistake I will ever make. Yet, although He knows the failure I may be tomorrow, He will never withhold a blessing today. He rewards faith whenever—and in whomever—He sees it.

Yes, we may question God's choice of Gideon, Sampson or Jonah, but we must remember that God calls men and women not only to work *through* them, but to work *in* them. He never makes a mistake. He always chooses the right man at the right time for the right mission.

How To Hide From God

Unfortunately, Jonah didn't see things God's way. The rebellious servant boarded his ship for Tarshish and quickly set out to sea. While millions run unknowingly from God, Jonah knew exactly what he was doing. From the outset, he vowed to hide himself from the presence of God.

Poor Jonah! He should have known it was impossible to run out of God's sight and reach. No matter where he hid himself, God always knew where the errant prophet was!

Oh, we may reach a period in our walk with God that we feel He has withdrawn His presence from us, but God is with us just the same. Every believer will endure a season of testing. We will be tested to see if we walk by faith or feeling. On the cross, Jesus cried, "My God, My God, why hast Thou forsaken Me?"(Mark 15:34). David wrote, "How long, O Lord? Wilt Thou forget me forever?

How long wilt Thou hide Thy face from me?" (Psalm 13:1).

But that feeling of existence without the presence of God is merely that, a feeling. Just as we teach our children to walk by moving a short distance away and holding out our arms, so God teaches us to walk by withdrawing the *feeling* of His presence. But He remains always near, always ready to steady, lift and comfort. We have His promise to never leave us.

King David realized the truth of God's omnipresence. He wrote:

"O Lord, Thou hast searched me and known me. Thou dost know when I sit down and when I rise up; Thou dost understand my thought from afar. Thou dost scrutinize my path and my lying down, and art intimately acquainted with all my ways. Even before there is a word on my tongue, behold, O Lord, Thou dost know it all. Thou hast enclosed me behind and before, and laid Thy hand upon me. Such knowledge is too wonderful for me; it is too high, I cannot attain to it.

"Where can I go from Thy Spirit? Or where can I flee from Thy presence? If I ascend to heaven, Thou art there; if I make my bed in Sheol, behold, Thou art there. If I take the wings of the dawn, if I dwell in the remotest part of the sea, even there Thy hand will lead me, and Thy right hand will lay hold of me. If I say, 'Surely the darkness will overwhelm me, and the light around me will be night,' even the darkness is not dark to Thee, and the night is as bright as the day. Darkness and light are alike to Thee.

"For Thou didst form my inward parts; Thou didst weave me in my mother's womb. I will give thanks to Thee, for I am fearfully and wonderfully made; wonderful are Thy works, and my soul knows it very well. My frame was not hidden from Thee, when I was made in secret, and skillfully wrought in the depths of the earth. Thine eyes have seen my unformed substance; and in Thy book they were all written, the days that were ordained for me, when as yet there was not one of them" (Psalm 139:1-16).

I've had to live through periods when I wanted desperately to feel the assuring, comforting presence of God. I can't imagine how anyone would want to live without it. But I do know that if Jonah truly wanted to separate himself from God, he didn't have to buy an expensive ticket for a long ocean cruise. He could have stepped outside God's will and presence right there in Israel. He could have disobeyed simply by going nowhere.

Once A Preacher, Always A Preacher

Already we have discussed two important factors in Jonah's coming depression: he was distressed by the call of God, and he willfully chose to disobey the commandment of God. But there was a third reason that finally pushed Jonah over the brink. On his way to a city where Jonah thought God couldn't find him, Jonah ran smack into God Himself!

"And the Lord hurled a great wind on the sea and there was a great storm on the sea so that the ship was about to break up. Then the sailors became afraid, and every man cried to his god, and they threw the cargo which was in the ship into the sea to lighten it for them. But Jonah had gone below into the hold of the ship, lain down, and fallen sound asleep.

"So the captain approached him and said, 'How is it that you are sleeping? Get up, call on your god. Perhaps your god will be concerned about us so that we will not perish,' And each man said to his mate, 'Come, let us cast lots so we may learn on whose account this calamity has struck us.' So they cast lots and the lot fell on Jonah.

"Then they said to him, 'Tell us, now! On whose account has this calamity struck us? What is your occupation? And where do you come from? What is your country? From what people are you?' " (Jonah 1:4-8).

It is one thing to run from Jezebel as Elijah did. It is quite another to run from God! He shook the entire sea just to reach one man. Whereas God sent a storm because Elijah prayed, God now sent a storm because Jonah wouldn't pray!

The wind of that storm rocked Jonah's ship

until the ship was about to break up under the pounding. Sailors scurried furiously to save her, but not Jonah! The prophet of God had fallen asleep. He had problems far worse than any storm.

Jonah's sleep gives us an indication of his mounting depression. It is common for depressed persons to sleep because sleep is an easy, temporary escape from reality. There are other escapes, of course—some may choose liquor or expensive shopping sprees—but when depression strikes, almost everyone attempts to run from it. Jonah ran to a seaport, to a ship, and now ran to sleep. He tried everything to escape the raging storm within him, but to no avail.

But though Jonah ran from God, he couldn't run from his ministry. As soon as the storm turned bad, his shipmates began to seek God. As the world usually does in times of calamity, they turned to a preacher for direction. Little did they realize that a backslidden prophet was the source of their troubles!

It was the ship's captain that first put Jonah on the spot. "Get up!" he said. "Call on your god. Perhaps your god will be concerned about us so that we will not perish."

As one who had once talked directly to God, Jonah could have easily explained how concerned God was at that very moment. He could have reassured the captain that God cared for the ship and every life onboard. Yet Jonah said nothing.

The last thing he wanted to do was talk about God, and we have no record that he did.

Finally the entire crew approached him. It was too late to duck the issue then!

"And he said to them, 'I am a Hebrew, and I fear the Lord God of heaven who made the sea and the dry land.' Then the men became extremely frightened and they said to him, 'How could you do this?' For the men knew that he was fleeing from the presence of the Lord, because he had told them.

"So they said to him, 'What should we do to you that the sea may become calm for us?'—for the sea was becoming increasingly stormy. And he said to them, 'Pick me up and throw me into the sea. Then the sea will become calm for you, for I know that on account of me this great storm has come upon you....So they picked up Jonah, threw him into the sea, and the sea stopped its raging" (Jonah 1:9-12,15).

It is in this passage of Scripture that Jonah finally reached his pit of depression. Now he had lost his effectiveness as a minister and all pretense of self-respect. He lost his sense of self-worth. As long as his turmoil was secret to him alone, he could endure. But once he was forced to face men who prayed to gods of stone and give an account of his failure, Jonah realized he was no better than his heathen shipmates, no better than the inhabitants of wicked Nineveh. In fact, once his shame was laid bare before all the world, he probably felt worse! He was stripped of dignity and pride, and brought to the lowest depth of despair.

A Pit Within a Pit

It meant nothing, then, to be thrown into the sea. Jonah had already determined he had no reason for living. Better to die, he thought, then bear such shame. Once he had said he was finished with God. Now, far worse, he felt as if God was finished with him!

If only Jonah had cried to his Lord from the deck of that ship! I'm convinced God would have heard him. But Jonah had yet to reach the place of repentance. He had one more lesson to learn before he could start back up from the road to depression.

He had to learn that God loved him even as he ran. Just moments after his head plunged deep into the sea, God sent a great fish to swallow him. Finally God had His prophet in a place He could deal with him one to one.

The Bible says that once Jonah hit the surf, the sea "stopped its raging." You can be sure, however, that a storm still raged inside Jonah's heart. Now it was a storm of complete unworthiness, broken by proof of God's miraculous love. I believe Jonah understood that God sent that great fish along not to devour him, but to deliver him to shore. The thought of such love must have overwhelmed him. He said:

"I called out of my distress to the Lord, and He answered me. I cried for help from the depth of Sheol; You did hear my voice. For You had cast me into the deep, into the heart of the seas, and the current engulfed me. All Your breakers and billows passed over me.

"So I said, 'I have been expelled from Your sight. Nevertheless I will look again toward Your holy temple.'

"Water encompassed me to the point of death. The great deep engulfed me, weeds were wrapped around my head. I descended to the roots of the mountains. The earth with its bars was around me forever, but You have brought up my life from the pit, O Lord my God. While I was fainting away, I remembered the Lord; and my prayer came to You, into Your holy temple.

"Those who regard vain idols forsake their faithfulness, but I will sacrifice to Thee with the voice of thanksgiving. That which I have vowed I will pay. Salvation is from the Lord" (Jonah 2:8,9).

"You have brought up my life from the pit." Jonah prayed those words from inside the stomach of a fish! The fish wasn't his pit. Depression was! But when he called out to God, he felt his depression drop free and his distress turn to praise.

What caused the release of Jonah's depression? How could he begin to speak praises to God? The next time you fall into the pit of despair as you run from the will of God, learn what Jonah learned. *Stop running!* It's as easy as that. The end of depression is as easy as surrendering yourself to God.

Jonah stopped running from God and found peace in the belly of a fish. His new spiritual beginning, however, didn't end his old responsibility. Jonah found that the call of God was still waiting for him. God had not changed His mind about Nineveh. Surrendering to God meant accepting God's calling, and Jonah finally consented. "That which I have vowed I will pay," he said.

If you've been depressed because you have shirked responsibility that God has given you, let me tell you where to find His presence again. Ask forgiveness, then go right back to the place you ran from and begin again. You'll find your calling still awaits you. God still has his right man for the right mission.

Remember, too, the great lengths God will go to convince you of His will. If He rattled Jonah's ship, He will rattle yours. He will call to you through circumstances. He will beckon to you through trouble. He will make it hard for you to walk away from the One who loves you with such infinite love.

Be thankful for it! The Good Shepherd will leave the fold to search the world for you. He offers us peace, challenge and fulfillment. There is no rest without Him.

If you've ducked out on God and now experience troubled seas, be thankful! The God of all the world is concerned for you.

Surrender to Him! Run to Him! Let Him restore you to the joy of fellowship that only His presence can give.

CHAPTER NINE

THE DEPRESSION OF DAVID

Few people represent success and prosperity any better than King David. From early childhood, he seems destined to succeed in life, as if he possessed a Midas touch that turned everything around him to gold. He was successful as a young shepherd guarding his father's sheep, and found instant fame when he killed Goliath, the Philistine champion. He became the closest friend of a king's son, and his personality and strength of character attracted followers and won the heart of Israel.

David was also a spiritual leader, a prophet and songwriter of national acclaim. No other king influenced Israel to fear God as much as he did. Under his leadership, Israel enjoyed her period of greatest blessing and achievement. It's no wonder the Bible calls him a man after God's own heart.

Truly David was a successful man, but even successful men are subject to bouts of depression. This mighty king is typical of modern Christians who become depressed because of past or present sin and its accompanying guilt. His life is a shining example for every man or woman who desperately needs assurance that God forgives even the worst in us.

Here's David's story:

"Now when evening came David arose from his bed and walked around on the roof of the king's house, and from the roof he saw a woman bathing; and the woman was very beautiful in appearance.

"So David sent and inquired about the woman. And one said, 'Is this not Bathsheba, the daughter of Eliam, the wife of Uriah the Hittite?'

"And David sent messengers and took her, and when she came to him, he lay with her; and when she had purified herself from her uncleanness, she returned to her house.

"And the woman conceived; and she sent and told David, and said, 'I am pregnant.'" David attempted to rectify the situation by sending Uriah home from the war to be with his wife. But when that failed he established a new plan.

"Now it came about in the morning that David wrote a letter to Joab, and sent it by the hand of Uriah.

"And he had written in the letter, saying, 'Place Uriah in the front line of the fiercest battle and withdraw from him, so that he may be struck down and die.'

"So it was as Joab kept watch on the city, that he put Uriah at the place where he knew there were valiant men.

"And the men of the city went out and fought against Joab, and some of the people among David's servants fell; and Uriah the Hittite also died" (2 Samuel 11:2-5,14-17).

Depression Should Lead to Repentance

Were David to visit me in my counseling room, I would hear the story of a man trapped in moral failure. He had betrayed his religious convictions through an illicit love affair with another man's wife. Now he was about to father a child out of wedlock. To make matters worse, he had tried to clean up his messy situation by ordering the death of his lover's husband, a loyal officer in David's army. With the husband dead, David thought, no one could charge adultery once the child was born.

When the details of David's sordid affair are laid bare, it sounds more contemporary to modern society than to ancient Israel. What a sad moral condition for Israel's greatest king!

I believe David became depressed because he knew what a horrible crime he had committed against God and man. Perhaps he felt convicted and miserable even in the act, but didn't possess the strength to stop himself. He saw himself as a wretched, wayward outcast, hardly worthy to be Israel's spiritual example. He felt intense guilt. He was hurt and ashamed, too dejected to face his God.

Men have been avoiding God ever since Adam first did it in the Garden of Eden. The knowledge and guilt of sin wants us to either hide the sin or hide ourselves from God. But hiding is the very worst thing we can do! How much pain and condemnation could we avoid if we would only go first to Him with our honest confession. Hiding our sin only deepens our shame and causes depression.

God did not create us *not to sin*. He created us to enjoy the fullness of relationship with Him. He made provisions for our sins. John the apostle wrote, "And this is the message we have heard from Him and announce to you, that God is light, and in Him there is no darkness at all. If we say that we have fellowship with Him and yet walk in the darkness, we lie and do not practice the truth; but if we walk in the light as He Himself is in the light, we have fellowhip with one another, and the blood of Jesus His Son cleanses us from all sin.

"If we say that we have no sin, we are deceiving ourselves, and the truth is not in us. If we confess our sins, He is faithful and righteous to forgive us our sins and to cleanse us from all unrighteousness. If we say that we have not sinned, we make Him a liar, and His word is not in us.

"My little children, I am writing these things to you that you may not sin. And if anyone sins, we have an Advocate with the father, Jesus Christ the righteous, and He Himself is the propitiation for our sins; and not for ours only, but also for those of the whole world" (1 John 1:5-2:2).

As long as we are human, we will sin. Though we strive to please God and avoid sin, we will occasionally fall. But instead of living in the fear of failure, it is important to learn where to turn when we do sin.

The Shepherd Meets the Prophet

It is when repentance is not forthcoming that Christians become depressed. Depression causes spiritual paralysis—when the heart is too ashamed to cry out to God, yet too wounded not to. There is no despair greater than the despair of a depressed child of God!

In our helpless and hurting condition, our heavenly Father comes to seek us out. He will explore every avenue to bring us back into full relationship with Him. In David's case the Scriptures do not specifically say that he was depressed. But because he had walked with God for so long, we can be assured that all was not well with David's soul. So God sent the prophet, Nathan.

"Nathan then said to David, 'You are the man! Thus says the Lord God of Israel...''It is I who anointed you king over Israel and it is I who delivered you from the hand of Saul. I also gave you your master's house and your master's wives into your care, ...and if that had been too little, I would have added to you many more things like these! Why have you despised the word of the Lord by doing evil in His sight? You have struck down Uriah the Hittite with the sword, have taken his wife to be your wife, and have killed him with the sword of the sons of Ammon."'

"Then David said to Nathan, 'I have sinned against the Lord.' And Nathan said to David, 'The Lord also has taken away your sin; you shall not die. However, because by this deed you have given occasion to the enemies of the Lord to blaspheme, the child also that is born to you shall surely die'" (2 Samuel 12:7-9, 13-14).

Nathan's words would have been useless had David not had a heart that feared God. But the truth from God pricked his heart and brought him to the point where he could confess his sin and be washed of guilt.

Truth and Consequences

It is important to realize, however, that even forgiveness cannot always alter the consequences of sin. What we plant we will harvest. David's sin affected others beside himself. Before it had run its course, his adultery would kill Uriah and an innocent but illegitimate child.

The child grew feverish and sick. "David therefore inquired of God for the child; and David fasted and went and lay all night on the ground. And the elders of his household stood beside him in order to raise him up from the ground, but he was unwilling and would not eat food with them.

"Then it happened on the seventh day that the child died. And the servants of David were afraid to tell him that the child was dead, for they said, 'Behold, while the child was still alive, we spoke to him and he did not listen to our voice. How then can we tell him that the child is dead, since he might do himself harm!'

"But when David saw that his servants were whispering together, David perceived that the child was dead; so David said to his servants, 'Is the child dead?' And they said, 'He is dead.' So David arose from the ground, washed, anointed himself, and changed his clothes; and he came into the house of the Lord and worshiped. Then he came to his own house, and when he requested, they set food before him and he ate" (2 Samuel 12:16-20).

Notice David's actions once the child had died. He acts as a man who asked God's forgiveness, who received forgiveness, and who forgave himself. How important it is to forgive ourselves! Forgiveness is never complete unless we have completely given the sin *and its consequence* to God. Unless we forgive ourselves, our guilt will grow into self-condemnation, self-contempt and self-hate. Satan will use it to destroy our usefulness to God.

We owe it to ourselves and to God to accept forgiveness, then to march forward by faith. The only thing that can make our sin worse is to allow it to rob God of our willingness and ability to serve Him. It deprives both God and us of fellowship! It deprives God of all He intended the cross to do.

Don't let unforgiveness of self rob God of you! Don't let Satan rob you of God!

Don't Forget to Forgive

David forgave himself. His experience is a beautiful example to follow in our own battle against depression.

First, David "arose from the ground" (2 Samuel 12:20). He repented, then left his tears at the altar. In so doing, he left his guilt and depression there. David rose from his sackcloth and ashes—from his place of repentance—restored to God.

Then David "washed" (verse 20). He cleansed himself. Our inward cleansing comes through the blood of Jesus the moment we ask forgiveness, but I also encourage you to make a visible, physical change that marks the end of your bout with sin. You may need to tear some provocative posters from your wall or toss out some compromising books, but put as much distance as possible between you and the sin that had bound you.

Third, David anointed himself (verse 20). Free from his encounter with sin, restored to fellowship, he then began anew for God. Past sin made him no less a servant of God. With a fresh anointing of the Holy Spirit, you, too, can walk from depression into a new dimension of God in your life.

After a fresh anointing, David then "changed his clothes" (verse 20), which symbolized his intent on starting a new life. God takes tattered garments and gives us robes of purity and righteousness. We must change our appearance, our outlook and attitude, and begin again as a servant of God.

Two further steps helped David conquer his depression. After changing his clothes, he *entered the Lord's house* and he *worshiped*. What better way to receive God's healing for the inner man than to spend time in His presence, time spent in a special manner of praise and worship? There our spirit is refreshed, renewed and restored. It is there the last vestiges of depression fall away.

The most precious element of forgiveness is forgetfulness. When God forgives, He forgets. We must forget the past as He does. Sins of the past must remain buried in the blood of Jesus.

It is God's desire to restore His children to fellowship. He does it as a father who waits patiently for a son to return home. His arms are ever extended, His table always includes a place for us.

Remember that the next time you sin. Remember, too, that He who has started a good work in you will surely bring it to completion. There need be no lasting failures with God.

CHAPTER TEN

YESTERDAY AND TOMORROW

I once heard a friend compare God's omnipotence to a man who stood on the roof of the country's tallest building, observing a parade far below. My friend said the crowd that huddled along the parade route represented humanity, while the parade was time itself.

According to the story, those small figures of humanity along the thoroughfare only saw the parade from a singular perspective. At one moment, every neck turned left, straining to catch a glimpse of the first lines of bright color. Minutes later, as the parade unfolded, every head turned right, watching the long column slip down the block to entertain yet another group of spectators.

But while the people along the curb watched the parade come and go, the man on the building saw things differently. He witnessed the parade as it assembled from the clusters of high school bands and pom-pom girls into a snake-like procession of marching feet. He saw portions of the parade still forming even as the first band turned its last corner and disbursed into a parking lot of yellow buses. While the crowd saw only small segments of the parade at a time, the man on the roof watched it all, from formation until completion, as if it were a single event unfolding before him.

My friend who told the story didn't have to explain the message behind it. I could understand that all events are either past, present or future. Like the parade spectators, we capture events in small segments, either *about to happen* or *as they happen*.

But God sees time as if from the roof of that tall building. He steps out of our dimension to view all of time in an eternal moment. He sees the parade forming and disbursing in a single glance. He knows where the parade began and where it's going, and understands every event it will encounter along the way.

He knows where our lives fall in the course of time, and every minute detail that will concern us!

How wonderful it would be to see things as God sees them! How fortunate it must be to see the thread of experience as it weaves the fabric of our lives, knowing what the finished product will be. But too often our finite perspective becomes preoccupied with one isolated set of circumstances, and we lose sight of our long-term purpose. It is when we begin seeing the parade of time from the street corner instead of the rooftop that depression is most likely to strike, either from concern over past, present, or future experiences.

Moses Looks Back

Our preoccupation with isolated events in our lives is like a forest ranger searching the colorful horizon with binoculars. Taken out of context, it is like colors lifted from an artist's canvas, futile to reveal the beauty of the whole. Trying to understand the purpose and reason behind isolated experiences can only distort the picture God is painting in us, and can only lead to unneeded worry, anxiety and—you guessed it—depression. After all, from our earthbound view of eternity, how can we know how the events of our life will work out in God's plan for us? The Bible says, "A man's steps are ordained by the Lord, How then can man understand his way?" (Proverbs 20:24).

Take, for instance, the case of the spunky sixth-grade boy who found a shiny new bicycle awaiting him on his birthday.

"Wow," he told a friend. "Now I can go anywhere I want to. What a good day this is!"

But a few days later, the little boy rode his bicycle into a telephone pole and broke his leg. All because of a birthday present! It wasn't a good day then!

Because of his broken leg, he spent several days in the hospital and was excused from final exams at school. Because of a bicycle! What a wonderful day it was to him then!

But with a broken leg, his parents cancelled his airplane trip to spend the summer with his grandmother and grandfather in the country. Months of anticipation melted into hot tears on his freckled cheeks. A bad day, right?

Yes, except that tragedy struck his intended flight, and over 85 passengers were killed. Suddenly the bicycle became the boy's salvation, a detail woven for good into his life.

An inconceivable story? Not at all. Our lives often meet with disasters that turn into blessings because we know that "God causes all things to work together for good to those who love God, to those who are called according to his purpose" (Romans 8:28). Psalm 37:23 says the steps of a righteous man are *established* by the Lord. In light of God's kind attention and guidance in our daily affairs, how can we know how God will work each day to our good until all the days are in?

Numbers 11:10-16 tells the story of a depressed people and their leader who had lost God's perspective. The Israelites had emerged from Egypt on a wave of miracles. God had opened the Red Sea before them, guided them with a cloud by day and a pillar of fire by night. He had made bitter water sweet at Marah, and when food was scarce, he had sent manna, a miraculous vitamin loaf that sustained three million Israelites in the desert for more than forty years.

It was a period of great victory for Israel. God Himself was leading them to establish a new kingdom where He would reign in their midst, bestowing unending blessings upon His chosen people.

But instead of their desert journey as a road to prosperity, greedy Israelites quickly focused their attention on the smallest of details—their appetites! "Who will give us meat to eat?" they murmured. "We remember the fish we used to eat free in Egypt, the cucumbers and the melons and the onions and the garlic, but now our appetite is gone. There is nothing to look at except this manna."

The complaints finally got the best of humble Moses. "Why have you been so hard on your servant?" he cried to God. "And why have I not found favor in your sight, that you have laid the burden of all this people on me?

"Was it I who conceived all this people? Was it I who brought them forth, that you should say to me, 'Carry them in your bosom as a nurse carries a nursing infant, to the land which you did swear to their fathers'?

"Where am I to get meat to give all this people? For they weep before me, saying, 'Give us meat that we may eat!' I alone am not able to carry all this people, because it is too burdensome for me. So if you are going to deal thus with me, please kill me at once, if I have found favor in your sight, and do not let me see my wretchedness."

Israel's problem, to be sure, was caused by unbelief and greed in the presence of Almighty God, but Moses' depression was caused by endless hours of hearing the complaints of a stiff-necked people. If negative, whining complaints could wear down the spirit of a man like Moses, we would do well to separate ourselves from them!

The irony of Israel's complaint to Moses was the beautiful references made to Egypt. To be sure, the desert was no paradise, but how could anyone compare it to Egypt? In the desert was hot sand, aching feet, rough beds and manna. But there was also freedom! In Egypt was the sting of a whip, grueling hours in the burning sun, rationed water and slavery. Surely the desert was the better place. The Israelites had prayed for freedom!

Now the root of Israel's depression surfaces. The people had lost their perspective. Instead of facing the realities of the day, they glorified yesterday! In the hot desert sun, they had forgotten the hot Egyptian sun. In the aches of walking to freedom, they had forgotten the aches of slavery. In the throes of momentary misery, they could remember only the good of a place they had so thoroughly despised.

How much like the Israelites we often are! In times of discouragement as Christians, we remember the good times before we met Christ, and our heart often returns there. We forget our hurt, our agony and loneliness without Christ, and remember only an oasis of fun. If allowed a place in our heart, that attraction to yesterday will bring depression. Our "good old days" can block our future for God.

But is yesterday really better than today? Certainly it wasn't for Israel, and probably it's not for us. Is yesterday really worth being depressed about?

I knew a minister who lost his wife in death. After some time, he began dating the widow of another minister who had died. The woman's husband had been dead for two years, yet she still wore black. As the minister and the widow dated, people began speculating they were serious about each other, but he confided to me, "No way! I don't want to marry a corpse!"

The woman couldn't let go of the past, and it sapped the joys of today. How tragic. If you are holding onto a corpse, listen to the words of Jesus: "Follow Me; and allow the dead to bury their own dead" (Matthew 8:22). Cut the past loose, and move out for Christ!

Whereas the people of Israel took their problem to their leader, Moses took his complaint directly to God. "Where am I to get meat to give to all this people?" he cried in frustration. "I am not able to carry all this people, because it is too burdensome for me." Moses' problem wasn't an overglorification of the past, but an over-emphasis of the present. True, God called Moses to lead Israel out of bondage, yet Moses was only the instrument. God was the real deliverer. And God knew all about Israel's problem and exactly how to correct it. He had everything under control.

But first things first. Before God dealt with complaining Israel, He dealt with His prophet. He gathered seventy upstanding men of the nation and treained them to assist Moses in daily leadership. Actually, He told Moses to take things easy, to stop taking too much upon himself. There was no reason for Moses to break himself physically and emotionally when He who kept Israel neither slumbered nor slept. Like so many of us, Moses forgot he worked *with* God, not alone.

Don't over-tax yourself in the press of daily living. Get some help. Even Jesus called twelve disciples to help Him spread the Gospel. It is good to lean on the arms of others, and rest our hearts in God.

Tomorrow Never Comes

In our generation, a look down the road can be even more depressing than a look over the shoulder, and certainly more frightening. Flip your dial and you will hear evidence of violence, famine, recession, inflation, and permissiveness—until it seems the earth is literally crumbling from sin. It's no wonder that young people are frightened and their parents depressed!

The only reliable fact in today's society is that

change is inevitable. One thousand generations traveled by horseback, but there are people who have watched us move from the carriage to the car to the moon in their lifetimes. In a hundred years, we have discarded the pony express and wireless for telephones, microwave, laser communications and satellites. We have moved from the farm to the city to share more knowledge and more change than we've ever known before.

And we have paid for our rapid change with a staggering loss of traditional values. We have swapped stable families for stepparents, foster homes and child care centers. We work longer and harder, but enjoy it less because money has become the bottom line of self-esteem. Economists tell us that one great strain on our society is the burden to maintain a standard of living we can no longer afford. So it takes Dad and Mom both working a job or two each to bring home the goods that Dad once brought home alone, and the quality of life itself deteriorates. Meanwhile, rising inflation rates and shortages threaten to wipe out the small savings few have managed to tuck away.

The tempo of time has created pressure even among Christians. Recently, one man approached me and said, "Pastor, if the Lord is coming so soon, why work? It's going to all be over soon, anyway." Young people, thinking the end of the age has descended upon them, rush for all the gusto they can get. They jump into ill-conceived marriages, hoping to know the satisfaction of a family before time robs them of the opportunity. Young men feel war is inevitable, so they drop out of school and wander aimlessly from job to job. In the distress of the times, millions have thrown up their hands and said, "What's the use anymore?"

Other Christians have tried to prepare for the events they see coming quickly upon the earth. Several years ago, one evangelist visiting my church painted such a bleak picture of the future that several career businessmen in the congregation backed out of business ventures and grew apathetic about life in general.

Such Christians fail to remember that Christ intended His bride to be the salt of the earth, poured out liberally in our communities to create a thirst for Jesus. Even Christian communes won't make the stress of life disappear. Stress will be with us until Jesus comes.

Until Jesus Comes

If we shouldn't be depressed by the news we constantly hear and see, why are events so depressing around us? I have news for you: *they aren't!*

Oh, it sounds bleak to read Joel's prophecy that there will be wonders in the sky and on the earth, blood, fire and columns of smoke. And I shudder to imagine that the sun will be turned into darkness and the moon into blood before the great and awesome day of the Lord (Joel 2:30-31).

But Joel gave us the good news first! "I will pour out My Spirit on all mankind; and your sons and daughters will prophesy, your old men will dream dreams, your young men will see visions. And even on the male and female servants, I will pour out My Spirit in those days" (Joel 2:28-29). There's nothing distressing about that!

Even Christ's long description of the end of the age was intended to comfort the Christian. "When you hear of wars and rumors of wars," He said, "do not be frightened; those things must take place" (Mark 13:7). "But when these things begin to take place, straighten up and lift up your heads, because your redemption is drawing near" (Luke 21:28).

He foretold us to forwarn us, to comfort us in advance. The Lord who cares for sparrows has seen the parade's final turn. And He is in control.

Why should the time of Christ's appearing find us troubled? Paul wrote, "For the Lord himself will descend from heaven with a shout, with the voice of the archangel, and with the trumpet of God; and the dead in Christ shall rise first. Then we who are alive and remain shall be caught up together with them in the clouds to meet the Lord in the air, and thus shall we always be with the Lord.

"Therefore comfort one another with these words" (1 Thessalonians 4:18).

We are living in a time of great spiritual conflict. Even the blind can see that our twentieth century world is cracking from the strain of sin. If we saw only the darkness, we, too, would despair.

But Jesus has given us a light in the darkenss. He has poured out His Spirit; He has given us a commission to work until He comes. He has shown us the future to challange us. "Whenever a woman is in travail she has sorrow," He said, "because her hour has come; but when she gives birth to the child, she remembers the anguish no more, for joy that a child has been born into the world.

"Therefore you, too, now have sorrow; but I will see you again, and your heart will rejoice, and no one takes your joy away from you" (John 16:22).

We are to live in joy. Christ's presence is full of it, "In thy presence is fulness of joy" (Psalms 16:11). A moment alone in His presence sweeps us from the gutters along the parade route and places us on the rooftop with Him. We can see clearly again. We can more fully understand that these times that trouble us only lead us closer to the day we will see Him and live with Him forever.

These are the last days. Wonderful, aren't they?

CHAPTER ELEVEN

DEPRESSING ASSOCIATIONS

As we've seen, even Moses had his problems with complaining, negative associates. In a desert of parched sand and cactus, they grumbled and questioned his leadership. When they mumbled, "Who will give us meat to eat?", they were really taunting him, as if to say, "Okay, Mr. Prophet, how are you going to get us out of this fix? Or will we have to find someone who can?"

Spiritual giants, of course, are only giants when they reach heaven. In this case, Moses was still very much human, and the belittling remarks he constantly heard cut him to the quick. Finally, he did about the only thing a besieged leader could do—he took his frustration to God. The Lord listened patiently—He had heard the grumblings all along—then He helped Moses in a way that serves as an example for depression victims today. God split Moses' duties among qualified administrators *to give him as much help as possible with the doubting, complaining multitude.*

Who Needs a Pessimist?

God had a reason for doing what He did. He knows that nothing deflates faith any faster than the needle of discouragement. It is worse than a burr under the saddle, more annoying than sand in a hiking boot, and always rubbing. Discouragement questions ability and leadership, erodes confidence and patience, and opens the mind and heart to sin.

Who needs friends like that?

Not every voice of discouragement comes from a malicious associate, of course. Most often, it is our well-meaning friends who do the damage. Through their casual, sarcastic remarks, they remind us of how *limited* we are. They love and want to help, but through discouragement, they often rob us. They rob us of the opportunity to push back our limitations, challenge life, and *win!* Oh, a word of encouragement is worth an ounce of gold to the heart that yearns to soar!

There is one prominent pastor who reacts to negative words in a very unique fashion. I've heard that when anyone gives him reasons why something can't be done, or degrades another person's achievement, this pastor turns his face toward the wall, crosses his arms, and sings to himself. He deliberately tunes out thoughts that bring discouragement, defeatism, or lack of resolve.

Like it or not, all of us live with natural pessimists, those friends or associates who think we're too little and too ordinary to accomplish anything of value. We rub shoulders with these pessimists daily, and if we're not careful, some of their negative attitudes will rub off on us.

What's it like to live with a pessimist? It's like a man trying to climb a mountain with a boulder strapped to his back. In the long run, the boulder will prove more dangerous than the mountain. Or it's like a woman shopping with a hole in the bottom of her cart. For every item she gains, one falls away. Pessimism will make the mountains seem higher and the achievements seem lower, if we achieve them at all.

A pessimist suffers seasickness during the entire voyage of life. I knew such a man in the Navy during World War II. As soon as the anchor rattled, he became seasick. Even before the ship moved, he knew he was going to be sick. So why wait? He got sick as soon as he heard the ship was putting out to sea.

Avoid the pessimist! He's the guy who blows out the candle to see how dark it can get.

Flowers in the Desert

The Bible is full of examples of these "dark cloud" friends, but none is more classic than the story of Job's comforters. These concerned souls traveled a far distance to cheer up a friend in misery, but they might as well have stayed home.

They brought him understanding, all right, but it was the kind that brought accusations instead of answers.

According to these sympathizers, Job's misfortune was the just result of hidden sin. Job only needed to confess his sin to them for God to smile again. Sound familiar?

"But I'm innocent before God," Job explained. "I have committed no sin."

"Oh?" one reasoned piously. "Just look at yourself. Is this the picture of a man blessed by God? You don't see me sitting on ashes scraping boils with a potsherd, do you?"

Even Job's wife had something negative to say. "Do you still hold fast to your integrity?" she scolded. "Curse God and die!"

Believe me, it's hard to live for Jesus when propped up by loved ones like those!

What a difference an optimist makes! An optimist can look at a desert and see a field of flowers. An optimist to a troubled soul is like a ten-yard head start to a sprinter. They give you the feel of winning.

Isaiah 41:6-7 shows optimists at work. "Each one helps his neighbor, and says to his brother, 'Be strong!' So the craftsman encourages the smelter, and he who smooths metal with the hammer encourages him who beats the anvil, saying of the soldering, 'It is good'; and he fastens it with nails, that it should not totter."

Caleb was an optimist—a man of faith. When he was 40, he joined eleven other Israelites sent to scout out Canaan, the land God had promised to give them.

Inside Canaan territory, the men paired off. Caleb teamed with Joshua, a close friend of Moses, and the two crept quietly through the Canaan countryside.

They saw everthing: the cities, the people, the orchards, the wells, the horses. They noted soil texture and water supply. As a precaution, they even logged possible resistance areas, in case they were questioned back at camp. With their notebooks complete, they hurried home, ahead of the other ten.

"It is a good land," Caleb said happily. "It flows with milk and honey. Good soil, good wells. It's a land of bounty, and it is ours for the taking as God has said." To every statement, Joshua nodded vigorously.

But as it turned out, the other ten were pessimists. They had seen the same land, visited the same cities, touched the same soil, but they saw a far different picture. They saw giants—giants who could destroy Israel, against whom normal men looked as small insects!

Hadn't Caleb and Joshua seen the giants? Of course they had! Weren't they men of reason? Certainly! But their reason was based on the reasonableness of God's promise. When seen through their eyes of faith, the giants of Canaan appeared as small as grasshoppers.

Caleb's optimistic faith was an attitude that steered his life. He still had it forty-five years later. When Israel finally entered Canaan, Caleb was one of the first to ask for territory. "I was forty years old when Moses the servant of the Lord sent me from Kadesh-barnea to spy out the land, and I brought word back to him as it was in my heart. Nevertheless my brethren who went up with me made the heart of the people melt with fear, but I followed the Lord my God fully" (Joshua 14:7-8).

Now he was asking for a piece of rocky hill country to settle as his inheritance. A pessimist might see that hill as an unlikely spot for a farm, but Caleb saw a mountain retreat with a panoramic view. He was unconquerable. He was an optimist.

Elisha was also a man of faith. When Elijah first found him, Elisha was plowing in his field. Plowing in rocky soil, of course, meant a farmer might have to hitch a pair of oxen. The stoniest ground might call for two pairs. But when Elijah saw him, Elisha was plowing with *twelve pairs* of oxen with a spirit determined to plow even concrete. He had an optimistic spirit, and God saw it.

"I can use a man like that," the Lord whispered

to Elijah. "Let's call him." And he did.

Walking Together in God

Notice that men of faith hardly ever work alone! It was Caleb and Joshua, Moses and Aaron, Paul and Silas, and Peter, James and John. No Lone Rangers here! Each of these famous men knew the importance of exchanging their thoughts, goals and insights with someone who could share their vision and faith. When one grew discouraged, the other picked him up. When one felt the strain of responsibility, the other eased the load. They were united in purpose and intent, like artists collaborating on a mural landscape. Each was strengthened, shaped and guided by the other's faith.

That's the way God intended us to live. In our marriage, work and recreation, we need companions who point us toward the potential God has given us. We need support. We need to hear the voice of encouragement from time to time.

Make it a practice to mark the person who discourages you, who leaves you feeling low, and shy away from him. Check your associates for those who hinder your faith, and side-step them. Ask God to direct you to men and women of faith, whose bubbling optimism will inspire you, whose presence alone will challenge you to be more than you now are for God.

Those friends are worth a million dollars. They

can help you overcome depression of spirit by nudging you closer to Jesus. Better yet, they can keep you clear of discouragement through that contagious outlook which is so characteristic of faith.

CHAPTER TWELVE

OBTAINING THE VICTORY

The Bible tells the story of four men caught in desperate times (2 Kings 7). They were diseased lepers banished from their homes to the outskirts of Samaria. By day they kept station together in the archway of the city gate, begging for coins and crumbs. By night they slept in a shack outside the wall. They were men marked for death by a disease that literally ate their flesh, a disease so contagious in those days that the law demanded they shout a warning to people who tried to come close to them.

In the best of times, the plight of these lepers was loneliness and pain, but this was no ordinary period in Israel's history. The four men had watched the Syrian army position itself outside the walls of Samaria to starve the city into surrender. Already a multitude of citizens had died, and the few who were left were eating anything they could put their hands on, even horses and dogs.

For lepers whose survival depended on a daily handout, times were especially bleak. Death by either starvation, leprosy or the Syrians grew in certainty every day. If anyone had reason to be depressed, it was these wretched outcasts, huddled in rags near the least secure portion of the city wall—the gate.

But it was in such desperate circumstances that one leper reached inside himself and found a morsel of faith. Leaning on his staff, he pulled himself to his feet and gathered his cloak around him. Then he turned to his friends, still sitting in the archway.

"Why do we sit here until we die?" he asked them. "If we go into the city where the famine is, we shall die there. If we sit here, we'll die anyway. So let's go into the Syrian camp where the food is. If they spare us, good. But if they kill us, well, we're going to die anyway."

It made good sense to the other three, so the men crept their way to the valley below Jerusalem and into the enemy's camp. There they discovered a miracle. Earlier that evening, God had frightened the Syrians with the sound of chariots. They had panicked and run! The Syrians were gone, but their camp was brimming with food and gold! All Jerusalem shared the bounty and celebrated. They were heroes!

What made the difference for four unnamed lepers? First, one had a heart that desired change.

That desire found a thimbleful of faith inside and gave him the courage to face reality. He realized his situation might never improve, but he wanted a different perspective, a brighter look at life. He wanted to be happy again, even in the face of death.

When he reached inside himself for that faint ember of faith, I am confident he felt the breath of God fanning it into a flame. God added to his faith and enabled him to step out for change. That divine faith helped him separate *conditions* from *attitude*, and enabled him to start down the road toward victory.

The attitude of this one unnamed leper centuries ago tells us how to shake depression loose today.

Depression at Road's End

Thousands of people suffer from what I call "end-of-the-road" depression. Their lives have unraveled from deep emotional or spiritual wounds they cannot fully understand. Sometimes their own failures create the circumstances that press upon them, but often they are the helpless victims of events they cannot influence or control. In any case, their mental and spiritual state leads them down a path of fear, great anxiety and self-doubt until it turns the last corner of despair. That's where these sufferers reach the road's end. The pain inside them becomes so intense, the emptiness and doubt so vast, that they must either solve their crises or find relief from the pain. If no answer is forthcoming, relief becomes the only escape, sometimes through alcohol, sometimes through suicide.

But I don't believe in dead-end streets! I don't believe in tombs to bury the living! I believe Jesus has given us all the tools we need to score a victory over this great killer, depression. I'm convinced we can beat depression if we understand these three important areas of life:

First, *know your enemy*. Is it physical, spiritual or emotional? Depression induced by physical symptoms can often be treated and cured by modern medicine or change in diet. If for no apparent reason you feel yourself losing vitality, consult a physician. Sometimes a physical tune-up can bring you into top form again.

But if the cause isn't physical, look into your heart. Often depression is a result of a spiritual wound that can be healed if we find the cause. We must understand that depression itself is not the wound. The cause may be deception, rejection, suspicion, or a host of circumstances that cause us to lose our self-reliance and joy. The cause may be Satan himself, who searches the world for those he can destroy. Hunt the cause of your depression, and face it!

Know your enemy! Don't fight blind! Save your strength for the culprit that robs you of your greatest resource—*your faith*.

Secondly, *know yourself*. Come to grips with your weaknesses, and find friends who will pray with you. Make deliberate changes that will help break your mental pattern. Perhaps you should rearrange your office, take a different route to work, or find a hobby. Try to understand why you have reacted the way you have, then seek to change. If your problem comes from sin or failure, be quick to ask God's forgiveness, and don't forget to forgive yourself. Root out the weeds that choke your joy.

Take Mr. Johnson as a case in point. His problem had begun when his oldest of four boys, Tom, was still in high school. Little by little, Tom had challenged the family rules: slipping out of church to cruise around town, smoking joints with the gang on a vacant parking lot on Main Street. Mr. Johnson reacted with firmness and fairness, he thought, but things only got worse. After graduation, Tom drifted from one job to another, staying out later and later, with each morning encounter between father and son growing in intensity and emotion.

Mr. Johnson was disturbed. He sought counsel and he prayed, but there was no evidence of change. Then one night the phone rang.

"Mr. Johnson? This is Sergeant Grant. We've got your boy downtown. He's doped out, Mr. Johnson, and he's just robbed a store."

This time, Tom had "crossed the line." Mr. Johnson paid the boy's bail, and the two took a long, silent ride home. But once inside the house, they broke into a shouting match. Mr. Johnson laid down the family law, hard and swift, but Tom wasn't buying. In anger, he ran out the front door, slammed the car into gear, and shot out the driveway, tires squealing. Tom rounded the corner and left his father standing, fist clenched, on the porch.

That was six weeks ago. There has been no word from Tom since. Every night Mr. Johnson sits up through the ten o'clock news, then turns off the bedroom light. But sleep doesn't come. A heart hurt this deeply doesn't sleep. Always his thoughts are of that wayward son, perhaps in trouble and needing help—perhaps even dead—and of the raging argument that split the family apart. Desperately he wants to find his boy and bring him home, but he thinks he may well be too late. He thinks he has failed as a father and as a Christian, and that nothing could ever make things right again.

Is it a sin to fail? Ask King David. Ask Jonah. Ask Elijah and Moses, and a host of others who failed in life. Though renowned for their companionship with God, each of these great men failed far worse than did Mr. Johnson. But they turned their failures into learning experiences, times of contrite repentance when they denounced their carnal ways to embrace the grace of God. Then they rose again and walked in a more satisfying understanding of God's love.

Is it a sin to fail? Of course not! It is a sin to quit!

Mr. Johnson had to learn that truth. He had to recognize that he had indeed failed as a Christian father. He had to accept his blame, but he couldn't live forever in personal disgrace. Fortunately, his broken heart gave expression to repentance. In his deepest anguish, he touched God, and felt again the peace that passes understanding. He found forgiveness and felt his guilt fall aside.

Then he forgave himself. He didn't like what he had done, but it was over and passed. He would change. He would apologize to Tom whenever his son came home.

Tom *would* come home, he believed, for when parental effort failed, God was still in charge. And Tom did come home. It was a loving father who prayed, but it was a compassionate heavenly Father who brought the miracle of restitution between father and son.

It is important that we know ourselves, acknowledge responsibility that is due us, then ask forgiveness.

Sadly, I've talked with many individuals like Mary Alice. After twenty years of marriage to a promising corporate executive, she had discovered signs of unfaithfulness. At first she looked the other way, refusing to believe what her suspicions were telling her, but eventually the dam broke. She confronted her husband with the evidence, and he readily—too readily—confessed every detail.

She wished she had chosen to live with the lies! But the truth was out, and she felt cheap and destitute and cheated. She had worked while her husband went to college. She had kept house and raised the family while he worked late and climbed the corporate ladder. Now, at forty-two, she faced a pending divorce with no skills and with a heart cracked open with pain and rejection. She was wasted and alone. Where could she turn when the world was so wrong?

Tragically, Mary Alice became her own worst enemy because she failed to understand the pain inside her. She lost her will to fight. She faced a choice between depression and the reality of rejection, and depression hurt the least. *She chose to live depressed.* Depression brought sympathy from friends and family members, and kept her from the embarrassment of being turned down for a job. Mary Alice didn't ask for the rejection she received, but because she willed not to face it, or to allow the Lord to heal her from it, she became depression's slave. She began drinking, until she became a slave to alcohol as well.

How important it is to understand the motives that drive us, and deal with them. Don't sit there until you die!

Most important in the battle with depression, *know your God*. How many of life's cares would fall helplessly aside if we could only see the vast love of our heavenly Father! We must join His perspective to see that problems are nothing more than spins on the potter's wheel. With each spin—with each trial of faith—we can be shaped more perfectly into the likeness of Christ.

"It is the blessing of the Lord that makes rich, and he adds no sorrow to it," reads Proverbs 10:22. The Jerusalem Bible says it differently: "The blessing of Yahweh is what brings riches to this hard toil, and he adds no sorrow or no depression."

Mr. Gary Jones quotes that scripture from memory since a brush with depression several years ago. Then he was a stable family man in his mid-fifties, who lived in a middle-class neighborhood outside a large Midwestern city. Mr. Jones had three married children and two granddaughters, and prided himself as a strong father and good provider. He had worked hard, paid the bills, sent the children through college, and had always made a way so that his wife, Betsy, didn't have to work. They preferred it that way.

Then came word that his employer, a giant chemical company, was moving south. All operations in the city would be curtailed, and administration personnel would be relocated. But Mr. Jones wasn't "administration"; his job was mid-management, and the company was making no plans for him. He could apply for a job with the company in the south, with no assurances, or he could find another place to work.

Actually, Mr. Jones had no choice. He couldn't bear to move a thousand miles from his children and grandchildren, and even then he was too old to put down new roots. At a time he was thinking more and more about retirement, he couldn't possibly purchase another home. The old homestead wouldn't bring enough money to replace it in the growing sunbelt.

Caught in a dilemma he couldn't avoid, Mr. Jones began looking for a new company. He was reliable, with more than twenty-five years of management experience. Why did the doors keep closing? Always the reasons were the same. Companies didn't want to pay his high salary when they could find and train young, energetic college graduates for much less money.

Day after day, the possibilities dwindled, while bill after bill piled up. Every mail delivery brought another bill and another worry.

It troubled him greatly when Mrs. Jones sought and found a secretarial job—he knew she had never wanted to work—but it hurt the most when the kids began sending cash to help them get by. His pride was wounded, and feelings of inadequacy changed his face into long, drawn wrinkles.

Within three months, Mr. Jones wasn't talking

to anyone, especially the members of his family. And unknown to them, his quicksand depression was leading him closer to the only solution he could see to save his dignity: suicide.

But in one last act of desperation, Mr. Jones cried out to God. That day as he searched his Bible for a word of hope, he happened upon Proverbs 10:22, "It is the blessing of the Lord that makes rich, And He adds no sorrow to it." His spirit leaped within him! He had found new hope! The God of blessing did not sow sorrow. Mr. Jones understood deeper than words that God knew who he was and loved him.

So it was that Gary Jones, who had prided himself as a good provider, learned that God was his sufficiency. His attitude improved. He became jovial again, and consequently, more attractive to potential employers. He found a new job and a new start.

David drew closer to God through times of trouble. Once depressed, he wrote, "But as for me, my feet came close to stumbling; my steps had almost slipped." Where did he find help? "When I pondered to understand this, it was troublesome in my sight until I came into the sanctuary of God" (Psalm 73:2,16-17).

It is when we bathe in God's presence that we dust off the cares of life. He knows us, loves us as we are, and never rejects us. As frail as we are, He remembers we are the children He created and loves (Psalm 103:13,14) and is quick to forgive. 1 John 1:9 says, "If we confess our sins, he is faithful and righteous to forgive us our sins and to cleanse us from all unrighteousness."

The promise of forgiveness is an ounce of prevention that can keep us far from the ache of guilt.

A Final Promise

Finally, remember that it is important to regard everyone as more important than yourself (Philippians 2:3). The effect of your smile, given just because another human being is *worth* a smile, can reach into a hurting heart with healing. Love fosters all the good qualities that put depression to flight, wrapped up in a simple greeting like, "My, don't you look great today."

The apostle Paul left us with one challenge that is certain to drive depression off our doorsteps. Paul encouraged us to think of excellence!

"Rejoice in the Lord always; again I will say, rejoice! Be anxious for nothing, but in everything by prayer and supplication with thanksgiving let your requests be made known to God. And the peace of God, which surpasses comprehension, shall guard your hearts and your minds in Christ Jesus.

"Finally, brethren, whatever is true, whatever is honorable, whatever is right, whatever is pure, whatever is lovely, whatever is of good repute, if there is any excellence and if anything worthy of praise, let your mind dwell on these things. The things you have learned and received and heard and seen in me, practice these things; and the God of peace shall be with you" (Philippians 4:8-9).

Depression can be beaten. The God of peace is with us.